PRAISE FOR A CONSTELLATION OF GHOSTS:
A Speculative Memoir with Ravens

"Laraine Herring has written a groundbreaking, breathtaking tour de force here, excavating personal and ancestral trauma as she blazes forth new possibilities for both narrative and healing. *A Constellation of Ghosts* is reckoning and revelation, deeply embodied, wholly visionary. This book is unlike anything you've ever read; this book will rock you to the marrow and leave you changed."

- Gayle Brandeis, author of *The Art of Misdiagnosis: Surviving My Mother's Suicide*

"Gripping in its honesty, *A Constellation of Ghosts* is an incredible journey of self-discovery, revelation, mourning, and healing. I am awed by the strength and courage it took to write such a raw, personal book."

- Rick Hamilton, filmmaker and director of *Seeing Glory*

"Laraine Herring's *A Constellation of Ghosts* endearingly broaches the borders between poetic prose and prose poetry—a vivid, insistent, lyrical memoir. Herring presses on our universal yearning to reconcile the curious pull of loved ones who have been gone for decades. Beautifully crafted, inviting, and playful, the book explores the imprint of family, one's own mortality, and the ultimate gifts of grief. Her unusual story—in which it doesn't even seem odd that ravens appear and speak—merges a lovely elegy for her long-gone father with the author's illness, the need to move on from a long-held grief, and the lure of letting go."

- Lisa Romeo, author of *S*

"What's the best way to grieve? We could conjure ghosts, write and re-write our stories, collect history, quantify, create rituals, let go of that balloon, promising us comfort, at long last. Maybe our fathers will become ravens and speak to us until we no longer need them. Maybe we can sing a death lullaby, somehow putting our grief to rest. Through time, from her father's quarantine and affliction with polio, to the horror of cancer, and myriad violences, Herring asks and answers the question of how to let go. She commits to it. A generous literary act."

- Jenny Forrester, author of *Soft-Hearted Stories*

"From the moment her dad flies from beyond death to land in her life as a raven, Laraine Herring's beautiful memoir embodies her familial ghosts with voices that sing a lament for generational conflicts, departures, illness and death. A brilliant book that pushes the boundaries of form, truth and language to a place that is wholly magical and illuminating. From a scholar of grief, *A Constellation of Ghosts* is a beacon for navigating loss that is nuanced and empowering."

- Rebecca Fish Ewan, author of the cartoon/poetry memoir
By the Forces of Gravity

"Written with grace and beauty, this haunting memoir weaves Laraine Herring's dual stories about her cancer experiences and grief over the death decades earlier of her father who's returned to her in the form of a chain-smoking raven in the midst of her illness. This is no ordinary cancer or grief memoir. Herring's prose shimmers as we journey with her through past and present in her deftly crafted linear and theatrical narratives that recount intergenerational trauma and ultimately love's expansive power to heal even after death. This complex work will linger with the reader long after the last page is turned."

- Christine Shields Corrigan, author of *Again: Surviving Cancer Twice with Love and Lists, A Memoir*

Also by Laraine Herring

The Grief Forest: a book about what we don't talk about

On Being Stuck: Tapping into the Creative Power of Writer's Block

The Writing Warrior: Discovering the Courage to Free Your True Voice

Writing Begins with the Breath: Embodying Your Authentic Voice

Gathering Lights: A Novel of San Francisco

Into the Garden of Gethsemane, Georgia

Ghost Swamp Blues

Lost Fathers: How Women Can Heal from Adolescent Father Loss

A CONSTELLATION OF GHOSTS

A Speculative Memoir with Ravens

Laraine Herring

Regal House Publishing

Published by
Regal House Publishing, LLC
Raleigh, NC 27587
All rights reserved

ISBN -13 (paperback): 9781646030804
ISBN -13 (epub): 9781646031054
Library of Congress Control Number: 2020951951

Interior and cover design by C.B. Royal Designs
Cover images © by C. B. Royal
Author photography by MII Ramona Swift

Regal House Publishing, LLC
https://regalhousepublishing.com

Printed in the United States of America

For my mother, Elinor, who is indeed, fine.

We all have two lives,
and the second begins
when we realize
we have only one.

- Confucius

1

Words were your superpower.

They helped you make sense of everything, but now multi-syllabic words from a different vocabulary circle the sounds you understand, vultures waiting to devour the corpse of your useless language. These new combinations of letters—*cytotoxin, angiogenesis, immunohistiology*—swallow the words you are familiar with in large gulps.

You begin to detach from yourself. The white walls of the gastroenterologist's office collapse like a file box into black velvet corridors. You see your husband but he can no longer see you. Your feet have been pulled to the velvet, your body stretched rubber, words bouncing off your skin.

Cancer
Referral
Stage
Malignant
Surgery
Now

Next, the corridors unfold into a labyrinth of rooms, stairs, doors—all brushed black velvet, devoid of sound. Your gastroenterologist is talking to you, and your husband is touching your hand, but you've left them. Their mouths are moving but the language is garbled, the bubbles of fish under water. Without the ability to understand, you reach your hands to the walls, soft and thick and sticky. Each step pulls your enlarged body forward. The floor is a conveyor, doing what it must.

Once you've arrived fully in the velvet underground, new walls erect around you—the white drywall adorned with gold-embossed diplomas disappears into the black fabric, and the world where you came from is shut behind clear glass. You realize you've left your clothes, but it's too late. Your stretched rubber body bounces slowly floor to ceiling, wall to wall, your pale skin naked and electric against the dark.

Your doctor gives your husband a referral to a colorectal surgeon and turns back to his computer. A Shadow-you remains seated in the office, calmly writing down the next steps before gathering her belongings to leave. Shadow-you is making lists:

- talk to your dean
- find a cat sitter
- tell Mom
- find substitutes for classes
- fill out FMLA paperwork
- tell—

And you realize Shadow-you is doing the same thing you did when you were seven and your father had a heart attack and all the grown-ups thought he would die within a year, even though they never told you that. They told you everything was fine, but your eyes saw their lies. Cleaved in half, his chest scarred, his Daddyness had disintegrated into bruised cells. You broke apart then, a seven-year-old fragment watching a seven-year-old Shadow-self making the lists that she believed would save her:

- tell extended family
- write eulogy for Dad
- take care of Mom
- cry all the tears out now

It didn't work then; your tears still swim behind the decades of fine, but nonetheless, Shadow-you makes the lists that will overcome this crisis:

- prep classes for two months
- set up auto-pay for credit cards
- find proxies for your committees
- update your will

You wonder if that girl-fragment and her girl-shadow ever found their way back together again, but there are now more pressing matters, such as learning new vocabulary words and finding the key and the door to leave this black velvet place. The dark labyrinth stretches behind you and the double-paned sheet of glass in front of you is smooth. Shadow-you is smiling, saying something to the doctor, cracking a joke perhaps, and your husband has retreated to his brain to figure out how to fix the rebellion of your colon cells.

Shadow-you leaves the office, credit card in hand, to pay for services rendered in codes. You don't know the language of codes yet, of billing and declining and remanding, but you will. Shadow-you has a string tied to her wrist that reminds you of the friendship bracelets you would make in the backyard of your North Carolina home before your father got sick, before you moved to Arizona, before he died, before you shattered and the abuser got in, before cancer, but upon closer look, the shimmering string stretches, a connective thread from her body to you in your strange velvet box, and Shadow-you is pulling you and your new house behind her like a carnival balloon.

You press your face to the glass, but it distorts, and the waiting room and then the parking lot and then your red Toyota constrict and slip farther away. Shadow-you calls your dean, makes an appointment, checks an item off the list. You've been leaning on the glass and when you back away, the imprint of your forearms forms a keyhole.

A raven appears between the panes, right leg shorter than the left, a lit Pall Mall cigarette clipped in its beak. You rub your eyes. Shadow-you in the passenger seat of your car is now a brush stroke in an impressionist landscape. The raven, blue black and iridescent, grinds its cigarette out beneath its claw and uses its beak to tap along the inside of the glass, edging your armprints with its tick-tick-ticks. When it finishes, it pushes the cut piece of glass toward you and you jump back as it lands silently on the velvet. The raven cocks its head, its right eye finding yours, and winks as it steps through the keyhole, turns back for the dead cigarette, and then hops to your bare feet.

You reach your hand through the hole and touch the exterior pane, the world on the other side of it increasingly unfamiliar. You retreat and the raven fans its wings and leaps to your shoulder and its cool breath raises the hair on your still-naked flesh.

You have no words for this.

The wind from its brief flight from floor to shoulder tugs the fabric from the walls into a shift dress, which wraps snug around you. Raven pulls a dandelion from beneath its chest feathers and tucks it behind your ear, its white fluff floating between you.

"I have been trapped between the glass for so long," it says. "I wondered if you would ever come for me."

You shiver and the dandelion drops seeds.

"Do you have a light?" asks Raven. "We might be here quite a while."

Shadow-you has arrived at the college where she works with the copies of her colonoscopy report and the referral note. Her dean will meet with her in twenty minutes, so first she'll scan the medical records, start to keep a file and make notes of questions, things to do, things to stop doing.

"Look at me not her," says Raven. "I'm the one you've been focused on for thirty years." The bird flits quickly, floor to ceiling, wall to wall, biting at the velvet until it becomes a branch, and then it perches and shrieks:

"I see I see I see from sea to shining sea that you have created quite a story for us to act within like characters in black box theaters and you have built it so that we have just three ways to end this show: I will go, or you will go, or we will go together.

"I'm the one you pressed between the glass like clover thinking you could keep everything the same stop decay and hold me hostage to your past, but, daughter, I too have things to say and miles to go but you have captured me and kept me from my death.

"Tell me, daughter, are you so attached to me that you will die as well or now that you are at your crossroads will you reconsider what you've held and toss it up and down and out so you can see from sea to shining sea what still can be? Are you ready? Shall we write a script?"

His unpunctuated speech unspools your throat. All you'd ever wanted was one more chance to talk with him and so you whisper, while Shadow-you is filling out forms and calling your mother and researching words, while her cells are eating themselves, you whisper old-new words, "Daddy! Yes, let's make a play!"

"It will be a cast of only four: you and me and my mother and my father, and we will speak until there are no more words between us," says Raven. "And then you can decide the ending."

You look behind you and the halls have morphed into proscenium and arch, a wide stage draped in black velvet curtains, a single blue-white spotlight aimed at the floor. Raven plucks a feather, slices at your flesh and dips it in your blood. "You go first," he says. "It's your story."

You take the quill and start to scratch on the stage floor. The spotlight finds you. Houselights dim. You pause, body stiffening. "I can't. I can't write the story that contains your exit."

"Tick tock tick tock," Raven says. "It's my departure or yours."

Daddy.

Shadow-you is talking to your step-uncle, a doctor, who is telling her about the daVinci machine that will cut her belly open and remove part of her colon and put her back together. Shadow-you writes notes, good girl, good student, but her hand is shaking.

"Tick tock. Write."

Me

I was doing other things when cancer came, and my father, thirty years dead, returned to me as a raven.

2

Does a ghost have breath?

I wake up asking this after undergoing a lower anterior resection to remove a two-inch malignant tumor from my sigmoid colon. The plastic tubing from the oxygen tank claws at my nostrils. Who am I breathing in? Who am I breathing out? Months after I'm released from the hospital, I will still feel the pinch of the tubing; I will still feel tethered to the single bed with the plastic sheets. I'm on the sixth floor at HonorHealth Scottsdale Shea Medical Center in the oncology recovery ward. My window looks out over the roof of the adjoining building. A small TV mounted to the wall gets a dozen channels, including an odd compendium of *National Geographic* videos of frolicking animals. I keep that station on in the background. I like the big cats with their big paws.

Every time a baby is born in the hospital, a soft lullaby is played over the speakers. There is no such marker for a death, which bothers me. Marking only a birth and not a death is whitewashing life. I don't say anything—a pattern I am realizing has not been useful—but each time I hear the soft xylophone music, I wonder how many people have died in between the births, and how many people are standing numb or relieved or exhausted or manic in sterile rooms beside the shell of a human who had mattered to them. If I were to die here, I would want a song.

Five incisions etch my belly, each carved out by the room-sized daVinci surgical robot named Eva who handled the bulk of the cutting and stitching, while my surgeon, swathed in light blue from head to toe, controlled her from behind a computer screen; my colon, glittering with malignancy, exposed to the air and enlarged on stadium-sized screens around the operating room. Robot kisses, I call the bites, and my husband will kiss each one as they fade from black and blue and red to gray to ash to shadow. Today, the day following the surgery, my abdomen is a paintball field of colors and I can't sit up on my own. In addition to being attached to an oxygen tank, I am tethered to a catheter, a steady stream of glucose "food" which, in the months past surgery, will turn me briefly into a pre-diabetic, and a morphine drip—time released of course so that I can't slip too far away.

Who am I breathing in?

Who am I breathing out?

I don't want the morphine, and they tell me I'm not using it enough so they will be taking it away from me tomorrow. I want to feel everything because feeling everything means my body is alive and fighting for itself. Pain tells me I'm still here. If I numb my body, what might it do and where might it go without me? I can't numb the pain without numbing my mind and I must remember everything. I am frantic to remember everything. I want to stretch into every cell, to run my tongue over every limb, every toe and finger, every scar and splash of cellulite I've tried to hide and whisper, "Hello. I see you. I am here now."

Singing bowl chakra music plays on my iPad while the big cats frolic in silent non-HD quality. The computer station to my right flashes its constant screen saver about the dangers of MRSA. The man in the room next to mine moans. He will moan for three days before he's gone. I won't know whether he died or was moved to another location. There will be no song to tell me.

I'm alone now.

My family has gone home to rest and I am supposed to snuggle into the balm of morphine, but I can't. Won't. Pain is its own narcotic, and its waves and crests are surfable once I find their rhythm. It's been seventeen days since I was told I had colon cancer. I have two masters' degrees, but prior to learning this news, unless we were discussing punctuation, I could not have told you the various functions of the colon. I could not have told you about the virtues of various kinds of enemas. I have had three colonoscopies in twenty-three days, a CT scan, an MRI, and a six-and-a-half-hour surgery. I have been under general anesthesia three times and drunk and vomited gallons of Miralax and Gatorade. I am emptied out.

I also had a pedicure, and I asked my hair stylist to cut five inches off my hair and add gold streaks in it so I would sparkle like fireworks. On my last day of work before going on family medical leave, a colleague said, "That's so you—about to go in for major surgery and you get your hair done." It may seem frivolous, but I love hair and I love fashion and I love presenting myself as art. I also didn't know what might happen next. Would I lose my hair? Would I get weaker? Would they find something in surgery they didn't see in the scan? Would I die in the operating room of some other undiagnosed problem?

I couldn't control those things, but I could choose to cut my hair before it fell. I could choose to sparkle in sterility. When I am removed from the catheter in a few days, the nurse who will help me walk to the bathroom will comment on my toes—each toe a different bright color. "I love them," she will say. "They match your cool personality." What I don't know the day after surgery but will know very soon is that those pre-op choices— perhaps wasteful to an outsider's gaze—helped me be seen as a person to a team of caregivers who treat dozens of people in the same green gowns in the same rooms over and over again. I needed to assert: *See me. Remember me. Help me.*

A white board hangs beneath the television with my name, Laraine Herring, written across the top. Today is: Saturday, March 11, 2017. The weather is: Sunny. 86 degrees. Doctor: Kassir. Nurse: Karen. And then a box filled with secret words I don't understand that tell the nurses what I can and can't do, eat, drink, or take. I stare at the letters and numbers—glyphs of many undecipherable codes that will surround me in the coming months.

The codes are a slammed door. They are about me, but I am

denied access to their meaning. The doctors are using my super-power—words—to alienate me, and I am furious and terrified that I did not anticipate that. With all of the possible tragic outcomes, I never considered the inevitable one: language—my always and forever safe house—could turn on me. Words will become paragraphs of horrors that keep the doctors on one side of the table and me, the one embodying the subject of the conversation, mute, unable to participate.

I'm surprised every time I catch a glimpse of my bruised belly. Had I really thought they could cut into it without leaving fingerprints? I turn onto my right side, away from the window, fire-shards of pain clenching my abdomen. I won't push the morphine button. Pain grounds me to the bed. The wide door is closed, and there is only me, thousands of dollars of flashing, beeping equipment, and a ticker-tape of MRSA warnings.

Oh, and, well, there are also the ghosts.

Thirty miles across town, in a hospital that is now part of the Honor system but was then Thunderbird Samaritan, is the hospital where my father died thirty years ago in 1987. There was no song to mark his leaving.

I don't remember what floor he was on, and I don't remember the name of his doctor on his whiteboard, which may have been a chalkboard back then, but I remember it was Friday and I was nineteen and I had been in the ICU waiting room all night with my friend Dex. Hours before, I was splicing film at the movie theater where I worked, sixteen miles and thirty years away from the operating theater where I will be cut apart and spliced together. I was preparing for the long night ahead of watching all the new releases to make sure we put the film together in the right order when I got the call I had been anticipating for eleven years, ever since Dad's first heart attack. "He's in the hospital. You need to come."

I had been preparing for this day since 1976—rehearsing eulogies and phone calls, trying to cry all my tears out before his final day so I could take care of everyone else. I have since learned this process is called *anticipatory grief* and that it is

9

common and that it doesn't help prepare me for grief in any way, not one bit. But I didn't know that yet, and when I left the movie theater and drove to the hospital in my orange AMC Spirit, I felt like I was falling into a well-rehearsed script. Part of me was outside myself, watching me drive the few miles north to the hospital. *You must remember this*, my self-outside-myself told me. *This is important.* I watched myself walking to the automatic doors, pressing the up button at the elevator bank, noting how dry my eyes were. It had worked. My planning had worked. The tears were used up. My mother was there, red-eyed and silent. At some point, a nurse asked my mother for the list of all his medications, which she had also anticipated and pulled from her purse. Dex arrived and we went to sit in a waiting room with black faux-leather furniture and a soda machine.

We waited. I don't remember why we didn't go see him. ICU rules were different then. Maybe we did and I don't remember. Even when I know I *must remember* I don't always. Dad had a DNR—a Do Not Resuscitate—order, but he'd collapsed at home, blood kissing the carpet, and my mother couldn't refuse to call the ambulance, and the ambulance, once called, could not refuse to come. Dad had anticipated this day as well, but his plans were thwarted and he was alone in a hospital room, the one place he vowed he would never die. He'd spent many years of his life in hospitals—from months in the polio ward in Wilmington, North Carolina, when he was seven to weeks in ICU when he was thirty-six after his first heart attack (*myocardial infarction* the doctors would write in their secret code book of words) to multiple bypass surgeries hoping to prolong the time until this long-anticipated day arrived.

Mom left to go take a shower and I was alone in the faux-leather waiting room. Dex had left because he had to go to work and I was lying on the couch when a nurse came in and said, "If you want to see your father while he's alive, you need to come now."

I have since learned how they know when someone is about to die—they look for blood pooling in the toenails, a catch-and-pause pattern in the breath—but at the time I thought she was somehow magic. I went with her—and I really wish I had gone to see him sooner, but if I did I have repressed it—and saw him thrashing on the bed, his head looking far larger than it should be. He was tethered to machines as well, which ones I do not know, but he'd been restrained to the bed at one point. I learned later he had been trying to pull the tubes out. Had been trying to die on his own terms. That's the thing about hospitals—they're not so keen on your dying, intent on attaching you to any number of things to make sure you breathe a few more hours. They don't ask you what you want. I am learning this as I lie in HonorHealth Hospital Scottsdale Shea Medical Center's oncology recovery ward. They do not ask me. They just do.

I don't remember if his room had a window. I don't think it did. I stood too near him and too far away. I have always regretted not crawling into the tiny bed with him and holding him, but we didn't do that in life and it felt invasive to do it during the dying. I didn't sing to him or put on his favorite music. I watched him drowning in air like a fish on a boat deck gasping for the water. Gasping for home. I felt the tears rising, the water swelling in my chest, but I held it tight, as I had been taught to do, lest I make anyone else uncomfortable with my emotions. He coughed and I coughed and I couldn't keep the ocean down entirely. "I love you," I said, which felt strange to say in the open room because we didn't say that much in life either, but we both knew it to be true.

His death was not peaceful. It was late morning on Friday. I was supposed to be in class at the community college where I had chosen to go rather than accept a scholarship out of town because I knew—had *anticipated*—that this day would come and I knew I would carry the not-being-here heavier than the being-here. I could live with delaying college. I could not live with missing his departing.

He tossed from side to side, still trying to pull loose the tethers. I was a tether. My mother was a tether. He was trying to cut us away too. Mom was still not back. I had anticipated this moment—he and I alone—and it had arrived according to script. His head fell back to the pillow. He pulled at the tape on his arms.

"It will be soon," the nurse had said. "Soon."

Exhausted, he inhaled jagged and exhaled loud and I caught his breath in my own fractured inhale and closed my lips around it as the machine's lines went flat. There was no beeping because he did not want to be saved. His mother had tried a lifetime to save him, to convince him to confess his sins to Jesus so he would be healed, but nothing came of it. When he was forty, he fled the weight of the saving, taking us two thousand miles away from North Carolina to the deserts of Arizona, and in his final act of defiance in a hospital room, refused it again.

There should have been a song. Maybe a few bars from Elvis—young Elvis, hopeful Elvis, *alive* Elvis—but there wasn't. There was only me, holding his breath in my lungs for the next thirty years.

I want to pull at my tethers—I want the catheter out, the oxygen out, the morphine out, the glucose drip out. I want to walk on my own and pee and poop and eat food with my teeth. I want to pluck my chin hair and stand under a hot shower. Each of those things will happen over the next few days or the next few months. The hole in my vein where the tubes lived will seal. My blood sugar will normalize. The robot kisses will fade and my elimination system will find a new pattern. These tethers will go, leaving me with the strongest, invisible one: the tether I connected to my father's ghost.

The big cats wrestle in silence on the television. My chakra music has ended and I can't quite reach the iPad because, you know, tethers. I don't know what comes next. Did they find more cancer? Had it spread? What is going to happen to me? No one will say anything. The surgeon will see me tomorrow, they say, as if only he can deliver the definitions of the codes they all must know. Maybe I will be able to drink bone broth on my own. Maybe they will cut me free from one of these clear plastic ropes. Maybe it has metastasized.

I do not want to die.

I need water. I turn to access the call button and I see my father, his breath still buried in my cells, has returned. I reach for his face. It must be the morphine. I must have hit the release by accident. He catches my hand in his and his eyes are the exact blue I remembered. He whispers something low—*say it again, say it again, I can't hear you*—but he's vanished, the jumble of his words dancing in my ear, the damp hot of his breath evaporating on my neck.

A Play in the Ancestral Realm

Raven

I remember you, my daughter, before you were you. I watched you grow beneath my wife's belly, felt your feet kicking the walls of her womb. Always running, you were. Always trying to get out, get away, but when you were born, you wouldn't walk. Not for three years. You sat and you crawled and you watched and then one day you got up and walked into the next room and closed the door.

That was you. And that was you in relationship to us. To your mother and me. We could come close but not too close. We could watch you watching us from your playpen, but from the very beginning you were a closed book and I knew then what I know now, you had taken on a burden that wasn't yours. You had come into the world not just with her eyes and jaw and my love of language and history, but you came with the ghosts that made us *us*. Had we known creating a child forged a link not just to the best of us but to the parts of us we wanted desperately to erase, would we have made you? Would we have anchored another soul with our ghosts? Maybe that is all human creation is—a stringing together of ghosts born from one flicker of love, one sigh of release—a way of tethering us all together so that we don't get lost in the dark.

You'd think I'd know these things now that I am here.

I remember you watching me when I was dying. I was back in the hospital, and I was in that damned pastel gown with the snaps and I wasn't conscious but I had never been more awake. You wonder about these things now that you have been in the hospital, I watch you I watch you. You. I watch.

You know you're close when you feel both limp and living. Your body is asleep but *you*—you begin to crackle and unfold

14

and you never realized how big you were, how much space you could have taken up, how much of yourself you could have shared. I wanted to reach to you, but my arms were shackled to the bed because I had tried in the night, unconscious though I was yes I was but still the part of me that transcends me had tried to untangle myself from this body—to remove the tubes and needles and silence the relentlessly squawking machines.

When you are about to burst with breadth and depth, you know it will only be a few moments, and you want to resist like how you, daughter, wanted to resist the anesthesia before surgery, but always it is stronger. It is a tidal wave at the edge of your consciousness and you surrender to it without trying to even if for a moment you planned to anchor your defiant feet in the shifting sand.

I wanted to reach to you but we had not been a tactile family—too much Lutheran, too much Baptist, too much discomfort with the messiness of flesh—but I knew in that final dermal moment that to touch the skin of another was to touch the face of the God I had long wrestled with, to touch the flesh of another was to hold the very miracle of the cosmos, that 98.6 degree fire threading through us all.

I wanted you to touch me too, but I knew the beeping scared you, the thick restraints on my wrists, the unconscious thrashing of my body that was trying to kick loose my soul. I was breaking free of my bone-cage at the same time I was reaching for you and the full moon tide was coming and I could taste the salt spray on my lips and she smelled of life and my body twisted and I tugged at my chains like a Victorian ghost but they were not chains at all only flaccid representations of the human hope of permanence.

The nurse had brought you into my room that morning, alone you were alone only nineteen nineteen, only alone, and she told you I was leaving and you watched like you had watched me from the moment you opened your eyes from your curl in the crib to your petulant high school pout to this instant where we found ourselves on opposite sides of the river. I watched your birth passage—thrashing and bloody and dark—and you watched my death slide and I wondered for a blink who was waiting for me to emerge, flesh suit shed, shimmering sparkle of dust and I wanted to bring you with me not to take your life from you no no no but to take my very best thing with me—my daughter my daughter I wish so much I could have stayed stayed could have saved. You.

So I struck a bargain like Robert Johnson—song and guitar at the Delta Cross Roads—just a little bit more time just a little bit you see my daughter my daughter she will need me soon but the full moon tide kept rising. It's heard this song before so much before that it has a response can I get an amen amen can I get an amen who wants to be saved I do I do who wants to turn it over now I do I do the tide is rising the salt is churning the undertow has wrapped its fingers around me and I have one second left to memorize your face no lines yet no lines no gray and I watch you swallow my tide lapping at the muggy air in the sterile room gulping your own rising tide back squeezing your eyes closed to hold the waterline at bay you are watching me still tossing on the bed you are watching me slipping out behind my lips into the fluorescent room you are watching me last gasp death rattle death rattle only the shaking off of the lost tendons that held me held me to my house my house my lungs my spleen my liver my kidneys my useless leg my heart my heart my heart how well you have done for all that you have suffered through how well you have done my daughter my daughter drink me in this moment our moment please please just a little more time I come to the Cross Roads I come I come.

3

I can't find my father in the cemetery. I can't find him in the backyard or at the dinner table or at the doctor's office. Every noun that I visit is without him. Every verb fails to transport. So I close my eyes, look there, and fall asleep into altered places.

I've come to the ancestral plane. Hoping.

Tree branches hide panthers and rivers spout rainbow fish. Capuchin monkeys dance in the branches of the panther-trees and their chirps wake the parrot, which had been hiding in the understory. The ground beneath my feet is soft and resilient. The sponge-like quality of the layers of leaves and moss is a pillow for my feet, but soon enough the sun, an oblong orange disk sliced into thirds by shadow, takes its place high in a violet sky and the pillow-moss grows tentacles and wraps around my ankles and holds me down. A mosquito lands on my forearm. Its eyes are emeralds. I don't dare flick it away. Sweat beads on my neck, and its itch travels down my spine into the dip at my hips and down the backs of my legs. I'm wearing a cotton skirt and a tank top and my eyes blink back tears at the orange sun's heat. The moss at my feet releases its grip just enough so I can turn around and see the rows of altars. I had been expecting tombstones.

I had been expecting too much.

Candles spring alive on the altars, glimmering shimmering yellow flame in cracked red votive glass. The low wind carries the scent of big cat, bird, and monkey musk.

I had been expecting too much.

I thought it would be like the movies, where a wizened elder would unfurl from a tree trunk and present me with a bauble that would hold the answers I seek (if first, only first, "you unravel the mysteries of your own questions, young seeker," the wizened elder would admonish with a wink). I would traverse the obstacles, nearly losing everything only to find what I was seeking was within me all along and the closing credits would roll. But there's no brass-laden soaring score to redeem me now. No a-ha moment when the audience magically understands the meaning behind the struggles and can relax, at ease knowing the heroine has suffered bravely and justifiably and has been redeemed through that suffering. Now, the audience understands, now we can love her freely. She has suffered for her wisdom.

This narrative is false. This structure is a lie.

I approach the altars, each one a careful assembly of a life. My paternal grandparents' flames leap highest. My father's shrine is shrouded in fog.

The moon shimmers off the backs of the jumping rainbow fish and the trisected sun illuminates the altar grounds. The moss around my feet releases a bit more. I don't understand the light sources. How do I behave if it is neither day nor night? And where is my wise ghost? My ancestor who has called me here? The mosquito flies away and my skin reddens and rises its farewell. Do I wait? Do I approach an altar? If so, which one? I've never read a story or seen a film where there weren't signs to follow, breadcrumbs to snatch up at the base of the witch's door, but here, among moss, mosquito, monkey, parrot, panther, rainbow fish, trisected sun and crescent moon, I can't discern what is symbol and what is solid. Maybe there's no difference. Maybe I'm in the wrong place, but that can't be because they called me here. Didn't they? Or in my arrogance to control my own fate, did I invite myself to their world and now stand indignant, mosquito bite itching, knee-backs sweating, at the rudeness of their failure to appear at my adolescent insistence?

I had hoped to find my father here, in the ancestral realm. I wanted to ask some questions. I wanted my bauble of enlightenment. But instead I find the moon where the sun should be and the dead, if they are here at all, are hidden in the moss and the spike of the mosquito. It's pretty, the flickering flames in the votive glasses, the cool moon and hot sun, the glimmer of so many wild eyes. My skirt sticks to the sweat on the back of my legs and I feel wrapped in cool cloth, a swaddled infant in a new world.

A branch snaps behind me and I turn but there's nothing but wild sounds, and the fish scales covering my eyes have blinded me with brine. I'm not ready. I was uninvited. I thought I could control the narrative in a world I didn't create. Foolish. I can't even manage the story of my reality.

A monkey steps in front of me and my heart twitches. This is it! My moment of connection, of completion, of closure. But the monkey reaches his old-man hand toward my face and as I turn my cheek to be stroked, to be embraced at last by my dead father, he snatches my gold earring and runs away, the moss swallowing his footprints before I realize I could have followed.

The moon takes the sun's perch in the sky and the sun lies down among the altars turning the earth golden brown. The candles flicker out. The mosquitoes rise up and the moss releases my feet. I can move, but I can't stay here and I can't go back home. I wanted to find my father, and in that greatest of cosmic ironies, maybe I have. I have found the trap I built for him where neither he nor I are free.

Raven

I float.

Fly.

For a blip I think I have made a bargain more time more time more time but I have not made a bargain I have made a commitment. They are not the same exchanges. There is no white tunnel no white light no shore that was devoutly promised to me no sweet by and by no meet me at the riverside no cloud cushions to rest my bones upon.

I float and I wait.

I float and I wait and I don't hurt. For the first time in my awareness I don't hurt and that is something that is cause for reverie that is trumpets and banners and the right hand of God. I had thought in death I would no longer be I could no longer be the construct I had embodied on earth. I had thought I would be a part of everything dissolving into trees and rocks and air but consciousness lingers or maybe consciousness is all there ever was. I don't know how to think about this anymore now that I float. Fly. I see I see I see from one sea to the other sea from the north to the south from the inside to the out I see I see I see and I don't hurt.

I pushed past my chapped lips into a mouth ringed with salt. I slipped out of my nostrils as easy as the Pall Mall smoke once did but I only float, a hovering wisp a lisp a limping leg a hammertoe a heart attacked. Do newborns feel this way? Having slipped out of one body into a new world having breathed through a tube a cord attached to another not unlike my own intubation my own feeding tube do they wonder where to go what to do?

I remember my body before polio bit it in two cleaved me from me and the future I had imagined. That body could float in treetops on swamp skins on pillow tops freshly starched and ironed. That body could bend—a triangle a rectangle a star— and kick off from the earth and catch pigskin between sweaty palms and land feather light on sandy soil running toward a goal line believing that crossing into the paint meant something believing that everything happened for a reason believing that I could be saved needed saving wasn't enough without resurrection and stigmata wasn't whole without someone else sacrificing for me. But he is not here the one who sacrificed the martyr the confessor the son. He is not here only me and I am floating and I do not hurt and I am seeing sea to sea and I want to tell you what is happening, daughter, though I no longer know who it is happening to.

4

Restart.

I'm going to try to write what is happening in a traditional essay format. I wasn't given any tools from teachers or preachers to understand a story that won't follow the formula. Maybe if I write in a familiar way, I can make sense of this new plot twist.

Restart. Take one.

"And that's what they never tell you," says my father-as-raven. He stubs out the cherry on his Pall Mall cigarette with his neon-yellow beak, cocks a flat eye at me and stretches his wings, feathers of jet black tinged with indigo. He's been dead thirty years, but the conversations, cryptic though they are, have continued. It doesn't occur to me to ask how a raven smokes a cigarette. It's not relevant to anything. I'm just glad he's there. He hops along the stone wall that surrounds my tiny back patio. A blue jay swoops, squawks; my father watches, wings alert, but the jay retreats.

What? I want to scream. What is it they never tell you? But I know he won't say, or can't say. It is September, the month he died, and even here in the high desert of Arizona, the air has crisped and the trees are releasing their yellows and reds. He struts to my dying honeysuckle plant. He doesn't have to say it because I know. I can't grow things. I do not nurture.

Ravens live in my mountain town of Prescott, Arizona, year-round so I never have to worry that Dad-as-raven won't be here when I wander to the back yard to feed the stray cats that keep coming—brown ones, orange ones, black ones. Even as a child, I set out food on the back porch for the neighborhood cats. "Don't do that," my still-alive-dad would say. "The cats will stay." But that was what I wanted—the cats to stay. To feel safe. To know in the cold that someone has thought of them. Why would anyone not want the cats to stay? He wants to tell me not to put out food now as I pour kibble into a ceramic bowl, but he doesn't. Some arguments are not worth transcending death.

Dad-as-raven is about to fly away, his gaze always looking to the clouds watching something just beyond my vision. I want to go with him. I want to hear the predicate to the sentence: They never tell you _____.

"You know," he says without speaking and I hate when he does this—gets under and into my thoughts and then takes over. I don't remember when I first allowed him to do that. I don't ask how he's lived as a raven almost as long as he lived as a man, and I can't bear the question of how long I have lived without him, but everything is different since my surgery and he knows it. I have gotten closer to him. Not him the bird, but *him*, the part of him the bird is watching.

Dad stays for me. I'm supposed to let him go. This farewell was supposed to happen many years ago. I have freed balloons into blue skies; buried letters to him; visited his grave; carried his photographs, his letters, and his golf clubs from house to house to house. I am the family storyteller, the family therapist, and I have not found a way to do what I tell everyone else to do. Release, release, release. But the question is so strong now—who will I be without you? Who will I be if I send you to the blue skies in the helium chariot? These are tired questions. If I were my own client I would fire myself. But that isn't really the question, is it? Not if I peel it back.

He's going to hop away—flying away is too clichéd, like the damn balloons that are supposed to help grievers let go of the very sinews that held them together. The balloon launch makes everyone cry, which is cathartic, but changes nothing. We know this. All the therapists. I worked as a grief counselor to try and find out the secret knowledge that would let me *let go*, but there was nothing and now Dad and I find ourselves in my backyard as autumnal equinox approaches under the coral gold sunsets that only Arizona skies can make. I am home but I am lost. This piques his interest and he lights another cig. I never see how—I just see the smoke, the filter, the ember. No one else sees him and that is okay.

It is undeniable now, the age that sketches my face. My eyes are still green, though I don't recognize my face. My nose is still a ski jump, my cheeks still rosy, but the fear that is lurking underneath my "I" has inked itself across my skin. Every morning when I dress I touch the scars on my abdomen: one, two, three, four, and the fifth one, the smile below my belly button where they took my colon out of the dark and sliced it apart, then tucked it back in, shivering and stunned, unprepared to be exposed to oxygen, to light, to a knife. That's one thing they don't tell you—the shivering lasts longer than the surgery. The shivering isn't about the air, the light, the knife—the shivering is about knowing at any minute it could happen again. One cell could switch off. One cell. And I wouldn't know the moment it happened.

"They said the cigarettes would kill me," says Dad-as-raven.

"They did," I say.

"But I'm right here," he says, his golf-ball-sized head surrounded by blue smoke. He's a giant corvid, much bigger than any around. Twelve pounds maybe, with a wingspan more like a hawk's than a raven's. Perhaps he is a predator rather than a scavenger.

What they don't tell you.

It's cold.

I'm shivering.

The layers I wrapped myself with are too thin to protect me anymore.

"I had no idea," I say, thinking back to the weeks Dad spent in ICU when I was eight, the number of times his chest was cleaved apart, his own shivering heart stunned and shocked. I'm hoping he'll finish the sentence, but he's staring again. The clouds have shifted into long silver fingers. "You must have been so lonely." I'm thinking now of the quarantined polio bed he lay in, the eight-year-old boy paralyzed, stuck and cold in the Southern dark. The blue smoke swirls, a tiny tornado, but he doesn't speak.

Sometimes, when I wake up I think I am still in the hospital.

Sometimes it takes a few minutes to catch my breath, to return to my body under my thin cotton sheet, to no longer feel the plastic sweltering sheets of the recovery floor, to land in my bedroom where I am not tethered to machines and fluids and catheter bags. It's over; it's not over.

Like grieving.

The stray Maine Coon cat with the fire-yellow eyes has arrived. She winds around my legs. I pull burrs from her fur, pick her up, and inhale the smoke smell of her neck. She's had enough, wriggles free and begins to eat. Dad-as-raven hops closer and the cat freezes, crouches. She sees him.

"You can't keep them," he says, and I know that's true. I can feed her, put out bedding for her, but she will go back to the trees, back to the fields, and one day she won't return. "It makes her more beautiful, doesn't it?" he says, and I pick the cat back up, hold her feet tight.

"Don't go," I whisper into her ear, but her paws contract as a flock of ducks fly low across the yard, and she's off.

I want to run with her. She is guided by an inner knowing. I thought I had that too, before the tumor, but maybe I only imagined it. Dad-as-raven stops inhaling, lets the smoke fan around his head. Was that what they don't tell you? That you're not special? That no matter how much you plan and how well you manage your time, you are no different from anyone else and you won't be remembered a decade after your death?

Isn't that what writing is ultimately trying to do? Cheat the inevitable? Make the pain and melodrama and love and loss all mean something? Is that what they don't tell you? That none of it means anything?

The nihilism I wore so proudly in my twenties is no longer appealing. I want the cloak of illusion—of a benign presence taking care of it all—of someone who is indeed the Grand Author. I rejected it so completely and now I wish for its truth, but it crumbles in my fist.

I'm not sure writing this out is helping.

What they don't tell you...

Is something sudden will happen to you and then you

25

will have one foot in an old life and one foot in a new one, your center unzipped for all to see—one scar, two scars, three scars, four—the fifth one will never go away, never go. I am not embarrassed by them. They don't shame me. I look at them and can't quite believe they are there, that I was gutted and re-assembled, and only the cells around the incisions remember, and they are dividing and dying and dividing and dying every day.

What is real? My father is a raven. I am holding a stray cat. She is safe. She is safe. I will keep her safe. You can't. You can't. None of us is safe. None of us can stay. I have held back for too long. My whole life I have been quiet, sitting in the shadow of you, hoping there will be sunlight—hoping there will be the place where I can shine.

This is getting very abstract and vague. How many decades have I taught creative writing? Be specific. Find the image. Return to the raven. The smoke. The soft purr of the cat. The cat that will be gone one day, no matter how much food you put out for it, how much you try to care for it.

Stop with the pronoun shifting. Am I *I*? Am I *she*? Am I *you*? These things are essential to the narrative. You must know who is telling the story so you can trust the telling. You must know who I am if I expect you to follow me to the end.

I am unzipped.

You are unmoored.

She is unsteady.

The cat winds around my legs. Dusk is approaching. Coyotes will emerge and the stray cats will scatter—driven to protect themselves in ways I cannot understand.

I am following you.

I am falling.

I am felled.

I am flailing.

I am failing.

I am following you, but you are not here, so who am I fol-lowing? I am personifying a raven, conjuring your voice, des-perate to believe in its permanence. I am writing our story so I can find my way.

What they don't tell me.

What you forgot.

There is no they.

There is no me.

I am getting closer to the answer and farther from my father. And I guess that's as good a place as any to start searching for the story. What do I want most? My father to stay or my life to move forward? That's where the tension lives.

The cat scratches the bark of the alligator juniper tree. My father flies away for the afternoon, leaving the smoke from his cigarette dancing in the honeysuckle pot. In the blue spirals I see the back porch of my paternal grandmother's house on Masonboro Sound in Wilmington, North Carolina. The waterway is still there, though the house has long been gone. I am shelling butter beans, wiping the sweat from my neck, but soon I dissolve into them—my father and his sister—and I am not even a sparkle in the narrative, even though the script I follow is being written by these children, by these parents, by the *ping ping* of the bean shells in the aluminum buckets and the long shadows of the pine trees.

The cat is gone. The raven is gone. I scoop out one more handful of kibble as the first coyote's wail breaks the twilight's silence.

Stay safe, I whisper to the absent cat.

Stay close, I whisper to my father. *Stay close.*

Raven

A ghost is not what you think it is.

A ghost is a commitment. A ghost is a breath exchanged and held. A ghost is a promise that love is not limited to form. I am formless and I am form and I am unsteady in this space of no pauses of views from sea to sea but I am not panicked. I am not afraid I see you I see you. I see. See. You.

I am here and you, daughter, are there, and how am I to make sure that you have what you need that you stay in your life when I knew how much this day would change you?

You think I didn't hear you crying in your room when you were eight after I had my first heart attack first attack of heart first attack. You think I didn't see the tissues in the trashcan the swelling of your eyes and you think I didn't know that you were anticipating this day that has come and that you were hoping you could prepare for it like the Girl Scout manual told you you should always do—only preparing for an overnight camping trip and preparing to mourn a heart attacked are two different things. Besides, you hated camping.

I hear a cracking open. Of an egg? A wound? A door? Is this where Peter comes and I am judged and juried? Look! A feather floating by! A feather black like ink like the ink you write your words with, daughter, black like the inside of a kiss like the center of a tryst like the earth that has fallen on my coffin. Oil sleek the feather, its rachis holding tight to silky vanes, my own veins emptied and distilled upon a metal slab. It hovers and I reach for it like I could not reach for you and when I catch it it becomes another and then another and soon I am a formless form of feathers black and inky sleek and silky stretching out to wings.

This can't be good. Aren't wings supposed to be white and fluffy, not black and shiny? White wings get to heaven get rewarded but fast-forward I have become a shadow of feathers standing on yellow feet striped with black. My eyes are flat and eager and my beak a black magnificence to behold my tongue my tongue my tongue oh yes I speak I caw I spout sounds again like you like I once did like those who still are living.

Hark, hearken, hark who goes there? I float I see from sea to sea from then to next I float I wait I see I chatter-chat-chatter to the moon but here comes someone else something else. Is it another floater another lingerer another father wrestling with the ties that bound us close?

Raven's Father

I died in the cornfield looking for you, son. I thought I spotted you, seven years old again, hiding in the stalks, giggling, eyes closed, thinking I couldn't see you because you couldn't see me. Funny, since you died and truly couldn't see me anymore, all I saw around every corner, in every car, behind my eyelids, was you.

Death wasn't what I thought it would be. Did you feel the same? I thought it would be obvious, or else it would be annihilation, but it was neither. It was like moving from one dream to another on one of those long nights where your dreams dance into dawn and they don't quite go back to the dark. There was a bit of a jolt, and then when I fell to the ground, I was surprised that it didn't hurt. I mean, my bones are so old I must have broken at least one of them.

I'm not sure how long I lay there. It was odd to see my own face, my unblinking eyes the blue of the sea—the same as your eyes, son. I couldn't hear you anymore, no giggling, and I couldn't even imagine you. For the first time since you died, I'd lost you. I didn't know what to do but wait, so I curled up in the crook of my own arm. When the paramedics came, I tried to tell them: *My son, my son. I have lost my son.* But they couldn't hear me. One of them flashed a light in my eyes, but my pupils didn't react. They loaded me onto a stretcher, and I had to scramble to hang on to my arm.

If I left the cornfield, would you be able to find me?

When they didn't turn the siren on, I knew. I slipped to the floor of the ambulance and tried to hold my hand but I'd lost my grip. The paramedics talked over me, over the sheet they placed on my face, and their words sounded familiar, but I couldn't understand them anymore. Their meanings faded like the sound of your voice.

I'd never been in the mortuary in the dark. I waved at Grady, the bow tie-wearing mortician older than me, but he just pursed his lips, touched his heart with his fingertips. There would be no autopsy. I was too old. Your mother wouldn't have allowed it anyway. No desecration of the body to interfere with the Day of Resurrection. Grady pressed the back of his palm against my forehead. My friend, Grady, I see you. Hello? He slid my body into the cold steel box, a tag on my toe. I leapt in before he could close the door and turn out the light, grabbing my ankle and winding myself around my calf.

Grady knew you too. He was working here forty years ago, back when the children were dying, back when polio was stalking us all.

I had left you here once, son. I will never leave again.

Raven

I was told there would be feasts and streets paved with gold and harps that sing and white white wings and mothers and fathers from way back when waiting and embracing and claiming God is good God is good God is good let us celebrate this homegoing. I was told there'd be a Peter at a gate with a list and a pen and there would be a counting an accounting for my wasted days. Maybe it is Peter sneaking up on me now while I float formless. Maybe it is Satan get thee behind maybe it is Jesus broken bloodied just like me. Who are you? I have been here only seconds only always I would like to do so much more than watch.

The sound I hear it is my name but not the name you knew me by, daughter. Not Daddy. Not father. Not Glenn. It is something else just sound just sound I feel it in the marrow of my formless form.

Oh, daughter, I am back.

Me

I don't let go. I was supposed to. I should have stepped back when the machines silently shrieked. I should have meant it when I said goodbye, Daddy, go in peace, Glenn, I set you free, Father, I know how long you have suffered. I should have touched your hand like my mother did when she returned to

31

the hospital, I should have meant it when I told you it's okay to leave I don't need you anymore I will be all right, but surely the newly dead can recognize a lie.

You're right. I had planned for this moment. I knew I would be the one to call the family and to write the eulogy. I knew all this because I scripted it in the third grade. I watched myself watching you stilling, last breath releasing, and I made myself look. *Remember everything. Do not let this slip away like he just did. Do not release this moment.*

And I thought I was being a good writer, a brave daughter, a person who *took care of things*, and I was all of that on the outside, but what I had really done was freeze. In the cold hospital room, I recited the appropriate script to the air, "Daddy, I love you, Daddy, you can go," but my body denied those lines. My body said:

Please don't go don't go stay with me I am not ready you are not ready I can't do this now.

And I saw that words can relay anything, but the body can only speak the truth.

My body said:

Daddy, I will keep you close. I will never release you. This will never be all right and I will mold this moment into the foundation of my life. I will tell your story. I will make them remember you. I will be the pallbearer, the torch holder, the faithful wraith who walks the cliff's edge waiting for the one who will never return. I will be the perfect Southern Gothic figure.

And because the body cannot lie, I set my life in motion that late eighties morning with its words, not the ones I whispered. I lied to the air, and I started a story where neither of us could be free.

Instead of losing you in that hospital room, I gained the weight of you in my belly, in my shoulder, in my throat. I gained your fingers on my clavicle. My voice became coated with yours. When I forced myself to leave the room, I held out my hand and you took it and together we started over.

5

Here is how to become a ghost:

1. Experience a recent trauma that begins the loosening of your skin from your bones.

1a. Don't notice that your skin has been loosened from your bones. Enjoy the pleasure of dropping a size without trying. Your new book, *The Grief Diet*, will be a bestseller. Equate the loosening of your flesh with success and progress. You're becoming the thin girl inside the fat body your grandmother always said was there. *Such a pretty face.*

1b. Try not to think of your father six feet under in the plot by the oleander bushes, his bones releasing his skin.

2. Notice that when moving through the world as a fat woman, you were invisible. As a thin woman, you are noticed, but not for your brain or your writing or your compassion. You're noticed for your boobs and your butt and you have no tools for this attention. You were the fat girl long before you became the fat woman. The thin woman is helpless, unarmed without layers of squishy flesh. You are beautiful in your hunger. Everyone says so.

2a. When the suave dark man notices you, the fat woman, who now lives inside the thin woman, is repulsed. But the thin woman, who could never wear the tight jeans and the sleeveless top she's now sporting, dances over to him and smiles.

2b. In the cold dark of his coffin, your father tries to hold onto his finger flesh long enough to call you on the phone. Long enough to tell you to stop. But he can't find the wires underground. The mouthpiece is missing.

3. Agree to go out with the suave man that you feel drawn to

and repulsed by. Don't realize that what you want most of all is not to feel anything.

3a. When he kisses you, it shimmies all the way to your toes and you decide it must be love.

3b. Your father's skeleton fingers try to push at the lid of the casket, try to get back to you, but you dance in too-tight jeans and you play house with the dark man and you can't hear the bony fingers knocking at your door.

4. Move away from your family and move in with the dark man. You cannot bear to be alone, but you think you have grown up and started living. You aren't wise enough to know that death and life embody the same skin—that with each new cell you generate, another one disappears.

4a. When you wind up paying for everything—the rent, the food, the gas—you decide you are a modern woman. You don't believe you are being played.

4b. Your father remembers he told you to never leave the house without twenty dollars. He is angry that he didn't live long enough to tell you that there were also men who would stay with you just because you had twenty dollars.

5. Be excited that you and the dark man enjoyed writing and think that you will be able to share this activity and support each other in it.

5a. Watch him throw a tantrum in your intro to fiction class when your work was received better than his. Listen to him tell you it was your fault. You were trying to humiliate him. You have no experience to compare this to. Maybe you did do it on purpose. Did you write too well to overshadow him? It will be decades before you learn the words:

Projection.
Gaslighting.
Bullshit.

5b. The mouthpiece is unattached to the telephone and it hangs upside down in your father's skeleton fingers like a bat. Or a regret.

6. Stop writing. *

> * You were never that good anyway, and it isn't worth
> the trouble. His rage scares you, so you meet it with
> silence. With complacence. With complicity. You
> don't notice your own rage bubbling in the cauldron
> of your empty belly.

6a. This isn't what you imagined your twenties to be like. This isn't what college had promised. But you cannot leave him now. You know what it feels like to be left and you will never do that to another person.

> 6b. "I didn't leave you," says your father, but there is no dial tone, no receiver, no plump skin at the cheeks, no bobbing Adam's apple at the throat. He is sinking, but he can't let go of the mouthpiece. There was so much more he had left to say.

7. Begin to steal from the movie theatre where you work. Small bills. Never too much. You're the manager, so you can write the difference off in damaged merchandise—a tangled Red Vine here, a molded hot dog there. Write off the food. It isn't necessary. Then you can pay for the things he wants—the nice dinners, the nice clothes. Then you can avoid the conflict and the fight.

7a. The dark man is upset that you work so much and is convinced you're having an affair. Your lack of desire for him must mean you are engaged with another.

> 7b. "I didn't have enough time to tell you everything I wanted you to know," your father thinks he speaks, but the mouthpiece is impotent and he no longer has a tongue. He has grown accustomed to the dark and has made friends with the worms that have taken his liver. There is beauty in their hunger.

8. Have an affair with your first love, whom you run into at the movie theatre where you work (so the dark man can have nice dinners, nice clothes). Your first love met your father years ago and you cannot resist that connection, that chance to keep

your father alive. Plus. Sex without the promise of violence is nice. When you lie next to your first love you can sleep. You begin to eat, two meals a day now, and the dark man calls you fat, your breasts banana tits, your ass Jell-O.

8a. You're a modern woman now. Going to college. Working. Having an affair and keeping your own apartment. Twenty is so very old. You will never be this old again.

8b. Your father was forty-six when he died and he finds that terribly young. He hadn't yet wrinkled and puckered. He simply stopped after years of almost-stopping. It was time to dissolve. But under the earth with his worms and his limp leg and limp mouthpiece, he couldn't leave the living dirt.

9. Duck when he throws the butcher knife at your head. "If I wanted to hit you, I would have," he says and takes your car keys and subsequently your car and leaves you alone in the apartment you are paying for. You make scrambled eggs and eat them without chewing so you won't change your mind.

9a. Put away all the dishes. Make the bed and clean the bathroom. Wash his clothes with yours in the communal laundry. Feel the urge to protect your skinny jeans from touching his as they tumble in the heat.

9b. The worms haven't come for his lungs yet and he has one last breath in him—the exhale he'd been holding onto because you were there in the beeping yellow room on the morning he died and he couldn't release it all because that would mean he would leave you and your mother and he was so very tired but he couldn't go so he held and the worms didn't understand how his lungs were pink and pulsing while all around the skeleton the flesh fell in silent chunks.

Still.

Mad respect from the worms.

10. Consciously eliminate all your options for escape. You cannot tell anyone what it has been like with the dark man. You have become one of the women you have always pitied—the one who stayed. Suddenly, your heart expands with compassion

as you realize that staying or going is not a black-and-white decision. It is not only about having resources or options or places to go. It is also about believing you deserve to have those options. You left your grieving family. You left your friends. You wanted to dissolve into the dark man and another life and you have achieved that. You always achieve what you put in motion, but you are not always wise enough to discern what you've started.

10a. The dark man quits his job at Sizzler after just a few weeks because it is beneath him. He is meant to be an attorney. He is meant to be wealthy. You are still cleaning up soda and popcorn from the floors of the movie theatres and you're now managing to pocket $200 a week in small bills so he can eat like he's rich.

10b. The exhale is pressing up against the edges of his lungs and he knows he will have to release it or he will burst inside the coffin. The mouthpiece is touching the gape of his nose cavity and he thinks he might be able to make a sound. The breath is climbing up his esophagus. There is no more time.

11. Eighteen months after your father died, you come home after class (no more writing classes, just literature classes, the words of others) to the apartment you and your mother are paying for so the dark man feels rich, and there is a message on your answering machine. "Sugar," your father says. "Get out." Beep.

(Gentle Reader: this is the part of the essay that is not a metaphor. Drink your tea. Feel it hot in your throat. Feel it coat your breath with steam. Look around your room. Is there a shiver beneath your yellow wallpaper? A silver shimmer at the window?)

11a. You don't leave then, but now you know you will.

11b. There is no more breath and your father is exhausted and his lungs are collapsing like ellipses at the ends of paragraphs and he thinks he can go now but…

12. You load up your car in the dark and you leave for an undisclosed location. You can walk away from it all except...

you reach for his voice:

Sugar.

Sugar.

Sugar.

...and catch it in a jar like a firefly. You tighten the lid and set it on the dashboard of your orange AMC Spirit. Your own bones rattle in your loose skin; the moon is a thin sheath, its cool blue light unable to illuminate either of you, specters now, conspiring in shared darkness and running out of breath.

Dream; February 20, 2017; the night before my diagnosis

I see you again like I haven't seen you since the weeks after you died when you would visit my dreams every night, sometimes leaving on a train, sometimes on a bus, sometimes just with a handshake and a tip of your golf hat. You are so bright I am blinded and I close my eyes and I open up to what I have longed for—you reaching for me instead of me reaching for you. You look well and I am struck by how healthy you are, how your skin shines life and your arms are thick with healthy muscle. I don't know my age, but I'm in bed in a fetal position and you come closer and wrap your glowing arms around me and for a moment I can't move. I feel your heart against my spine and it's true in that moment that you have never left and then your hand is on my belly and you are placing something hot and yellow—a lava rock or a beating heart—into my womb and my belly opens to accept it and swallows it before I can look at it further and when I turn to ask you what it was, you're already in the corner of the room, your light folding in on itself until you are an origami dragonfly with shimmer wings.

"I think you left that behind, Sugar," you say and you are gone and I am in the dark and I wake up and I turn to my husband and say in sleep-wake,

"This must be bad. Dad is back."

Raven

I flip I flap I fly from sea to sea I see I coast and hover and somersault and I don't hurt. I should tell you there are others of us, black birds pecking, black birds gathering, black birds pairing. Did you know did you know did you know, daughter, that ravens mate for life? My wife, did she, does she know that I am back? I don't know the rules. Not yet. I only had a feather that became a body that became a beak that became me and now I am a raven and I wish I wish I wish I could tell her to wait for me I am back.

Maybe you could tell her to wait? I know you see me. I know you've kept me.

When I fly I remember what it was like to run along the sand by the creek in North Carolina when I was a boy. I thought I could fly then—leaping into the air to catch the baseballs the footballs the Frisbees—I thought I could fly and then the night came when polio bit my nervous system when my spine went to sleep and the heat flushed inside my skin. Flying was for dreams, I learned. Flying was for fools.

I am no fool I am no dreamer I am a survivor I am more than a boy lying with the dead in a room with iron lungs I am more than a boy who thought the world would be kind to him would bring him glory glory I am more than a boy. I see I see I see from sea to sea and there I am still wrapped in hot packs in a sweltering white room with no radio there I am able to see no one not my mother not my father not my sister though she snuck once to the window to wave at me while I was quarantined, separated, isolated there.

There I am hearing the words of the preacher a man of God—caw! caw! caw!—whispering over my not-yet-dead boy's body, "Lord if this child is to do your work, please spare his life. If he is not, then please spare another." Caw! Caw! Caw! I see that man blue eyes flat marbles I see that man cold hand on my cheek I see that man righteousness burning in his throat I see that man and I will rip out his heart now that I can fly.

Daughter, maybe I have returned for me.

6

I never noticed how much electricity was in hospital rooms. How much our living depended on currents coursing through cords. Philosophers talk about the spark of life, the flame of passion, the fire of anger. Science tells us energy can neither be created nor destroyed and mystics tell us we're the ash of flaming stars. After my father died, the electricity kept flowing. The machines recorded numbers plummeting toward zero.

Zero. The shape of an egg. The shape of life. Zero. A number and a digit that is neither positive nor negative. Zero. A placeholder. A wait-and-see symbol. A hold-on-dear-one-for-a-moment-or-a-lifetime—a just-wait-and-something-is-going-to-appear-here symbol. The zeros on the heart monitor, the zeros on the blood pressure monitor, held his place, his space as the temperature lights slowly decreased. The countdown:

98.2

98

97

Normally, the machines would cry as the numbers plummeted, but my father had an advanced directive so no one would come to answer the screaming, no one would shock his body with joules—electric hope electric salvation electric resurrection. He'd had enough current. He'd had enough resurrecting.

The room was cold. All the electricity must heat things up. I heard my heartbeat in my eardrums, my crying echoed in my ribs, my mouth a zero, a placeholder, a hold.

Raven's Father

Son, when I arrived at Masonboro Baptist Cemetery, I was still clinging to my dead leg snug inside the simple prepaid pine box. I could see through the wood and also down into the dirt where all the worms were waiting. That sounds awful, doesn't it, but it wasn't. Seeing such a perspective was comforting—like observing the inner workings of an old timepiece, every part working together to move a day forward.

Grady, my old mortician friend, had come out to see me laid to rest. He wore a top hat, and the cold rain dripped off the brim. There's that new preacher, who I never really got to know since I quit coming to the church once you died. But he's a good man, doing his duty, standing in the rain under the moss-trees, putting another one of us errant congregants in the earth. I hope he doesn't say I'm resting with Jesus because it's clear to me now that's not what's happening.

My great-grandfather was a founding member of this church, and everywhere I look I see the stones that marked our lives. Back during the World War I days, I remember Mama and I coming to lay flowers down on her mama's grave, a bouquet of roses or a simple branch of pine. "These are your people, son," she said during the handful of times I ever saw Mama cry. When I asked how grandma died, she just wrinkled her nose and pulled at her dress sleeves. "Life killed her," was all she'd say. My stone was already waiting. They just had to inscribe the last date.

When I was a boy, I'd climb these thick-rooted trees and dangle over the tombstones. I see a little glimmer right now of that—me in my overalls hanging by an arm and a leg, daring the dead to wake up.

I see some folks hiding in the branches, but I can't recognize them. Grady pours a shovel of dirt on my box and I have to make a choice. The preacher is walking away and the gravedigger, who'd been hanging back by the toolshed, is coming closer. You're not here, son. They buried you in the west and so this grave is not yet home.

The coffin starts to lower and without thinking I let my dead leg go and stand on top of my box. I am tall, son, and my arms stretch as wide as the earth. I didn't think I could let that flesh go—my home for eighty-one years—but as it cooled it became less of a home and more of an artifact, a curiosity to be studied under glass. Mama was right. These are my people. All my people but you, son. There's Mama with a rose, holding out her hand.

My gosh, son, all of life is all here all the time.

There's that dish of orange Jell-O marshmallow salad that Aunt Bea brought to every homecoming dinner. Bea's long gone, but there's that Jell-O, still shimmering in the dish. There's the preacher that baptized you, son, back in '41. His hair's not gray yet and he's still got all his teeth. I think he passed sometime around '78. I can't quite recall. All the seasons are here at once—the white and yellow of spring, the purple of summer, the red of fall and the dust of winter. I can't remember what season it was yesterday when I fell in the field and died and I don't think it matters. Son, the watch is a lie. Time doesn't move forward. It perpetually unfolds.

7

My paternal grandmother was as closed as winter, and when she spoke she expected you to know what she had been thinking and she expected you to do as she'd been expecting. I tried to choke down her rules along with the sweet tea and the good news of the second coming. I tried to smile enough but not too much, to play quietly and not complain about the heat and the mosquitoes, or the cold and the food, but I wasn't so good at it. My house, 200 miles west in Charlotte, North Carolina, was modern. It had plumbing, electric heat and cooling, a refrigerator that wasn't referred to as an ice box. My house didn't smell of canned figs and molded fruit. My house didn't have skeleton keys in doorknobs or oily placemats with tiny Confederate flags and cardinals on them.

I cannot remember a time I touched her voluntarily. Her voice cackled and creaked when she talked and her words had edges of judgment and ridicule. Her hair went prematurely white, so she always appeared old to me, more so than in the way that a person over thirty always appears old to a child. She was from *a different time*—a time when there was only outdoor plumbing. A time when the chickens on the farm became food. A time when a virus—*poliomyelitis* to be precise—crept into the small Southern town of Wilmington and infected my father, and that infection leeched into his sister, his mother, his father, and ultimately into me decades later. We didn't have the illness, but we had the repercussions from it. We had the energetic tendrils that came from Dad's years in isolation; years learning to reuse a limb that had fallen asleep like Sleeping Beauty; years fighting to live when everyone told him he would die. My father's sleeping limb made him lopsided. Made him lurch to the right side when he walked. But he could walk, and that made him an angry winner.

Polio had invaded Wilmington in 1949. The grown-ups had stopped telling children stories about the bogeyman or ghosts that wander through the woods. They stopped making jokes about what happened to bad girls and boys who didn't clean their plates or say their prayers. Some families went so far as to splash sheep's blood on their front doors so the Angel of Death might pass on by, leaving their boy or their girl one more day above the earth. Dad's family didn't paint the door, but they should have, because something fierce was walking through the town and no one saw it coming and no one saw it leave. Each time a little girl or a little boy was buried, a whirligig of pine needles stirred up, spinning as if making a tiny magic carpet to carry the baby souls away.

Poliomyelitis was an exceptionally hungry thing. It slipped into gutters and slid into gardens and fed the vegetables that the children ate. It sprouted wings from water fountains, white and colored, and slid over young lips, stilling the shivering dance at the base of their tongues. It floated through breaths of congratulations at Little League games and its tentacles wrapped around tiny ankles on hopscotch courts, shot stingers up the backs of calves playing Double Dutch, and settled in the bowls of hips, licking clean the last drop of soup.

Poliomyelitis hung upside down in the trees where children swung from their limber arms and it slithered down the ropes and onto their skins. It lay underneath the fallen leaves and layers of pine needles until someone stepped on it and with one strike, it took the child's leg. The child couldn't recall where he had stepped, no matter how many times the doctors asked him. He could tell them where he had walked on that last day of walking, but he couldn't point to that precise piece of earth that had speared him, so no one was able to catch it and carry it out of the town and release it into a different neighborhood, a different family, a different brother.

Polio means gray. *Myelon* means spinal or nervous tissue, and *itis* means inflammation. When you break the word apart it seems fixable, like a mosquito bite or a bruised shoulder. It seems controllable, pliable even, but the danger of the word lurks in the first part. Gray.

No one called it poliomyelitis. It was just polio, sometimes *infantile paralysis*, always whispered as it stole the colors from the children, turning them to soot and smoke, inflaming the hearts of those who lived through it, implanting a hidden rage thumping in their chest cages that shook them far far away from the roots that had been thick and solid. Polio splintered and paralyzed and suffocated. Its stealth fingers stole the children one after another, sometimes in mid-breath, leaving the untouched ones stuttering, searching for God in the harsh light of the new mourning.

I lay with the dead twice, my father wrote almost thirty years after he'd been stricken with polio, months after he'd had his first heart attack in 1976, resulting in the second time the doctors told him he would not live. *I lay with the dead twice,* he wrote on yellow legal paper, *and it made me damned mad.*

He was trying to write his story. He was preaching at the Salvation Army, punctuating his talk with a scratchy 33 rpm Elvis gospel album. He was still trying to find the God he was taught loathed him enough to cause his illness. Still trying to understand what he'd done that was so unforgiveable. I can't find in any of his papers where he found the answer.

After his death, I saw my grandparents once. They did not come to his funeral. My grandfather had shrunk six inches, and he now stooped, the top of his head barely clearing my own. My grandmother wore the same red lipstick and strand of pearls, and her voice had the same sharp edges. Skeleton keys still sat in the locks above the beveled-glass doorknobs; oily placemats with Confederate flags still protected the table.

Dear Daddy,

I looked for you in the house, in the bedroom where polio found you, but you were gone. No pictures of you on the walls. No mementos on the dresser. I could only feel you when I looked at your parents—your absence embedded in their bones.

Love,

Laraine

Aside from some emotional scars, I beat polio, my dad wrote in 1979 for his Salvation Army sermon. If I'd have been his writing teacher, I'd have circled that introductory clause and said, "Here! Go into here! What's swimming under those words is eating you alive." But of course I am not his writing teacher. I am his daughter, and I also excel at writing sentences that skirt the edge of truth.

Here are some:

After some bad choices in my twenties, I found gainful employment in academia.

And

I had a challenging experience with my second lover.

And

I have adjusted to living in the desert.

And

I have learned how to deal with loss and I release what I no longer need.

And

I am not angry.

"I'm not angry either," says my father-as-raven as he looks over my shoulder, his heart bloodied and pieced back together, bypass after bypass. His dark wings raise with each breath, revealing the interstate of scars across his breast.

"What was it like for you?" I am more desperate than ever to talk with him about illness now that I have been in surgery, now that I have been given A Diagnosis. Now that I go to the lab every three weeks.

"Daddy always told me you had to learn to be sick," my mother said after I was released from the hospital. But I am not sick, I think. I will not claim that word. Words become sentences which become stories which become lives which become obituaries.

There's no time for anger, but anger doesn't pay any attention to what I want and sets about gnawing at my cells anyway. It has to eat if it's going to stay, and it has to stay until I see it and I will never see it, never admit to it, at least not until I have given my name a dozen times to the well-scrubbed staff on the pre-op ward and I am lying in my own green hospital gown surrounded by fluorescence and sterility less than an hour before surgery, only sixteen days after I found out I had stage 2 colon cancer. The irony of the colon, the organ in charge of letting shit go turning on itself, isn't lost on me, but I'm not dwelling on that. The thought that won't shake loose as I rub my plastic ID bracelets together and watch the first drops of anesthesia slip into my vein is *what have I refused to feel?*

Me

I thought nineteen was an adult.

In the hours after you died, we went to Burger King. We drove through, of course, so no one could see death perched on our shoulders. I was in the back seat of your car behind my mother who was practical and prepared and we must surely eat so I ordered a chocolate milkshake and drank it in two gulps. I would spend the next two years eating mostly peanut M&Ms and drinking Diet Coke. I would lose sixty pounds, reaching a weight of 95, a weight that finally earned me the approval of the doctor, a weight that finally got me noticed by the boys who'd before only wanted friendship. I'd go to the mall—malls still had stores in them then—and I'd reach for the size I always was—a 12—and I'd step into the jeans and they'd fall to the ground. Every time it happened, I was surprised. Every time it happened, I'd look in the mirror and see angles in my round face, hip bones where there'd been flesh, a collarbone dip where there'd once been smooth skin. I'd try another pair. Size 8. Size 6. Size 4. Size 2. One more month and I could be a size 0. A placeholder.

Iceberg lettuce. M&Ms. Water. The occasional slice of pizza.

It's important that you know I wasn't doing this on purpose. I didn't decide I would starve, restrict, get skinny. I didn't decide I was fat or ugly or wrong. I simply wasn't hungry. No bingeing and purging. No counting calories or measuring my steak by the millimeter. I didn't have skinny-girl pictures taped on my mirror. I just had no desire for food.

It is easy to shrink when you no longer yearn for space.

My body had acted on its words *I will be the pallbearer. I will be the faithful wraith.* And the words even my body couldn't bring itself to say but nonetheless were etched in my cells, singing out my prophecy: *I will come to you. I will find you. I am so close to disappearing.*

In the hours after you died, after Burger King, I did exactly what I'd prepared to do: I called friends, called family. I convinced my mother's brother to come from Chicago even though my mother, steadfast, claimed she needed no one. She, like me, was oldest-daughter-capable.

I needed someone, though, and it was clear your family wouldn't come.

That is the thing I can't forgive.

Even thirty-one years later. Even after my own cancer woke me up. Even after decades of therapy.

How were there no plates of fried chicken and layers of your favorite chocolate cake at your funeral? How could not one of the souls who had made you make the trip from North Carolina to see you buried under one of the few oleander trees in the Phoenix desert? Not mother, not father, not sister. All were healthy. Wealthy.

But they did not come for you.

And they did not come for me.

I cannot forgive.

I am over fifty now.

I cannot forgive, and that anger has settled in my cells and turned them against me.

Raven

Daughter, I think my anger lodged in my attacked heart.

My epitaph says, "He walked by faith," but the truth is I walked with rage. Each step above the ground a roar from shore to shore. I hear your rage and raise you mine—see still it sparkles still it shines whether it is flesh or feather it's divine.

And yes, I would have enjoyed the chocolate cake at the wake that wasn't. I would have licked the bones from the chicken at the dinner-on-the-grounds you didn't have. I would have drunk the sweet tea like it was nectar from the gods and I would have sung of golden shores and glory be.

All the people at my funeral came for your mother and came for you and only a few came for me—golfing friends, mostly— my life was never here my life in Arizona was never mine it was a placeholder a zero a bridge between North Carolina and my death a place for you and your mother to make a life without me without me I knew you'd have to go without me.

We scraped the money together for you to fly home to North Carolina in the summers after we moved because you yearned for it like nothing we had ever seen before. We had not anticipated your need your pain your refusal to adapt. I had known I would not make it work could not make it work too many years in another place too many dreams in another space too long too long walking on a different earth.

But you did not adapt and you did not adjust and you did not forgive us for taking you away from the place where you were born for removing you from home. We thought we hoped that home could be as easily built on desert sand as ocean beach we made a choice we felt was best but underestimated just how Southern you'd become. I misjudged how deep our place had made its way into your bones and you have not forgiven us and you blame my family for closing the door for forgetting about you but you forget because you're blind to this you forget that it was I who made the call.

You forget it was I who chose the West who hoped for the best who hoped a future would unfold for you that you couldn't see yet that you couldn't imagine you forget it was I who chose because to remember would be to turn on me and you can't begrudge me my choice because I was ill and now I am dead and you can never overpower the shadow of death you can never speak ill of the ill of the dead.

Yet I too would have thought someone from home would have come. I would have thought my parents who'd feared I'd die from polio would bear witness at my passing. I would have thought my mother who wept alligator tears on the pier when I told her we were moving to Arizona would have come to see me off I would have thought my father who loved me loved me loved me would have come but maybe when I left I also left them abandoned and uncertain left them wondering what had gone so wrong between us that I had to go.

I see I see from sea to sea and nothing is like I had expected it to be though it must be like it was meant to be meant to be to be.

I don't yet know what I am, but I suspect I am in between. I was on my way into the tide choosing at the Cross Roads releasing my last rattled breath, but you called me back, daughter, and I am just trying to understand where I am and how this works and I think a part of me must not have wanted to go or else I'd have flown and become white winged silky not black winged oily flap-flap-flapping at the edge of everything.

Daughter, I think we have all never forgiven each other.

Raven's Father

I'd never been in the cemetery at dawn before, but I have to say, son, it's a beautiful place, so full of life you'd never expect. I can hear the music of the worms undulating under the earth. They never stop. A nest of sparrows is in the tree branch above me, their triangle beaks open to the sky. One of the eggs has fallen and cracked, its yolk stringing across the tree's roots. There's a garden snake underneath the azalea and so many squirrels you'd think the whole place is an oak. I can hear all the creatures breathing, their hearts pumping, their eyes blinking. It's not overwhelming; it's just the score of life.

It's cool and damp this morning, but that will change once the sun gets a bit more above the Atlantic's edge. The light is extraordinary—a buttercup yellow—dusting everything with gold. I'd fallen asleep on the mound of dirt over my coffin, still needing to be close to my body, but as the dew burns away, I feel like I can start walking.

I haven't heard any trumpets or harps or choirs, and I don't see a white light or a tunnel. You'd expect that would be dismaying, but it's not. I'm thinking that none of us saw the same things when we came into the world, so it's not very likely we'd have the same experiences when we leave it. I'm also thinking that it is harder to have a religion if everyone has a different afterlife, if everyone has their own redemption song. The part of that Bible story I wanted was you. I wanted to walk up to a golden shore and find you waiting for me. There are so many songs about that sweet by and by, it feels like the biggest betrayal of all not to see that river, not to hold your hand.

I remember our last conversation. Do you? You'd bought plane tickets to visit in October for Homecoming. We'd have eaten our dinner right here in this cemetery, where we had services and songs every year. Where our living and our dead said hello. Long distance was expensive, so we never talked much, but because you died, I remember what I would have otherwise forgotten.

"Are you still working out at Airlie?" you asked, and I said I was. Groundskeeping that old plantation gave my hands and my heart something to do.

"I broke par last week," you said, and I knew that was a big moment for you. I knew it had been months since you felt well enough to go out to the golf course. Months since you had a good round.

"Laraine is on her way over for lunch. She's nineteen, you know. I don't know how to talk to her anymore." I hadn't known how to talk to you for nearly that many years, son.

Your mother was tapping her Timex. The phone call had gone on too long, even at weekend rates.

"Well, son, I'll see you shortly," I said, and we hung up and I went out to the cornfield so I wouldn't start a fight with your mother.

There's a net around the cemetery, like a spider's web, and the air shimmers in it. I push against it and it stretches enough for me to slip through. When I look back, I see the cemetery pulsing with sound and light, encapsulated in silk. In front of me are specks of stars on velvet black, beneath my feet a rutted hardwood floor. The cemetery shrinks as I step forward and soon it is another star glinting in the sky.

I didn't say I love you, son, but you knew, right?
You knew?

8

I don't know my people, and maybe this is why they haunt.

When I was twelve, we moved away from North Carolina to protect my father. I know that now. We moved to provide me with a better opportunity than I would have after my father died if we'd stayed. But mostly we moved because my father's family was relentless in their dogmatic attacks on him. They were Southern Baptists. Prosperity Gospel folks, and they believed my dad's illness was due to his not being right with God. Video tapes and books and pamphlets showed up on our doorstep imploring him to confess and find the light again. Dad had nowhere to turn from this abuse, so we went West, where people have been going to reinvent themselves for centuries.

My mother's mother was an alcoholic and I only saw her twice in my life. My standout memory is of her teeth in a jar on the bedside table next to an open bag of plain M&Ms. My mother's father enabled his wife, and I also only saw him twice in my life. They lived in Bay Ridge, Brooklyn, in the same apartment my mother grew up in, an entirely different universe from suburban Charlotte, North Carolina. My mother loved her father fiercely. I do not think she loved her mother. She says her mother never once told her she loved her, even on her deathbed. I've no reason to doubt this.

I am envious of my students' papers on their extended family. Their love of cousins, aunts, nanas, and papas. I couldn't relate. I wouldn't recognize my cousins if I passed them on the street and my grandparents, all dead now, live in my memory as smells and clips of voices. When I was diagnosed with cancer, I wondered what it would be like to have extended family around me—grandparents, aunts, uncles, cousins—filling the room with balloons and flowers and music. My mother visited. My husband too. But most of my time in the hospital was spent alone until my dead father first returned and set up a permanent home in my psyche as a raven.

Liminal states of being, such as undergoing surgery with anesthesia and receiving life-changing information like a cancer diagnosis, are ripe periods for engagement with our ghosts. *Hello, death,* we say in these moments. *Is this how you will come for me? For so long I thought you would be nameless. A brush against my cheek at night. A hand around my heart. Something Gothic and romantic and distant. But here you are now, in my body and my bed, not romantic in the least. You're formed of genes and cells and ICD codes and survival statistics. You're a whisper when I had been so certain you'd be a shout.*

Death rarely responds.

But our dead scream.

"I'll come back and haunt you," I say to my husband, and I mean it. I want to do it. I want to be the spirit holding on, lurking in the closet between the sweaters, tapping people on the cheek with cold fingers, making them wonder. I want to reach smoky fingers into their ears while they sleep and tickle their dreams, then rearrange items on bookshelves and curl up at the foot of staircases and leave handprints on bathroom mirrors.

At least I thought I wanted this.

I have realized two things:

1) I have contributed to my father's ghost hanging around for thirty years. My spooky Southern fantasy of longing and yearning played out against a backdrop of moss-covered rotting plantations was nothing but the shadow of attachment. An inability of me to say: I will never see you again. Nothing but my way of getting in my own way—of holding on to an ideal, to a hope—my attempt to trick impermanence into permanence. The harder I hold, the more I ensure my own entrapment.

2) My father's ghost is not at ease. I held him here, but he also couldn't bring himself to leave. His wife, alone; his daughter, adrift. When he returned to me in that dream, he was golden-strong, not an angel, nothing so pedestrian and expected, but nonetheless an essence that woke me up and said in

unequivocal terms: *I am back.* To which I whispered to myself: *I never let you go.*

There's an old saying I remember from childhood: *Don't look back unless that's the direction you want to go.* All I do is look back. I'm a professional holder-on-er. Of everything. When I received the polio vaccine as a child, the pediatrician told me to put the liquid in my mouth. I did. He came back in five minutes and it was still in my mouth. He hadn't told me to swallow, so I held. The most natural thing of all.

I'm so good at holding on that I won't let go of being the person who is so good at holding on, even when cancer appeared. Even when my father reappeared. Even when I know in the dark of my bedroom in the middle of the night when I wake up wondering whether a new ache in my shoulder or a new bruise on my skin is a recurrence, that I am holding my own chains.

Cancer is a commitment.

Still, my raven-father screeches in my ear. Still, I see him fat and feathered in the corner. Still. I am still. Holding instead of moving. Pretending I don't hear the crying, that I don't know that I can help him find his way. Knowing when I do, he will fly away and become something else.

I don't even know who I'm holding on to anymore.

Go away. I don't want to talk about it anymore.

Daddy, I don't think I remember you.
I remember me remembering you.

Raven

My wife, your mother, had gone home to shower just a minute just a minute away and I took my moment my moment but I didn't know the nurse would bring you in. I had already started leaving the tide was pulling the sea was pounding at the levee of my bones. I didn't know I'd have to go while watching you watching me. I didn't know I'd have to leave you open-mouthed, dry heaving on the Lysoled floor. I'd have waited I would I would I would have waited so you didn't have to see me going from father to phantom in a wink, so you wouldn't have to carry more of my unfinished life than I gave you at your birth, so you wouldn't feel you had to carry a torch for me forever.

But. I also knew you'd been planning for this day since 1976, writing it into being, rehearsing it in front of your mirror, strawberry lip-glossed pout under heavily kohl-rimmed eyes. I'd stamped you with this day and you would have done anything to be here for it you did do everything to be here for it gave up scholarships to college refused to look at out of state schools let us be disappointed that you stayed so close to home went to a community college kept your high school job stayed so close to home but you did it all for this moment my moment our moment that we'd been hurtling toward for nineteen years. You did it all so you wouldn't have to let me go. You were greedy for my final moment. You'd have knocked down the nurse to be here. You'd have not showered for days to be here. You'd have waited watching me watching me and what could I do but give you your prize your defining storyline your point of no return what could I do but anoint your crown with my death my blood filling the inkwells of your pens my breath your muse your jailor your confidante your keeper? What could I do but go? It was what we'd agreed upon since the first breath I saw you take.

A father is a commitment.

Me

It's true that I had written about your death long before it happened. I dramatized it and took the stories of it to school so I could find a way to talk about it without talking about it. At home with you everything was fine, was always fine, but I heard you shuffling up and down the hallway when you thought we'd all gone to sleep. I heard you talking in the dark on the porch to the gray cat you swore you hated, saw you gathering futile hope with herbal supplements and hydrotherapy. I saw you stiffen and stumble when the polio you thought had left your body announced its final act in your back muscles, an *et tu* stabbing, a patient murderer who'd hibernated for forty years. I heard you tell my mother you would put a bullet in your head before you returned to a wheelchair, before you lost your legs again.

So I did write your death alive, or rather your dying. I left for high school in combat boots and a trench coat in the hot dark Arizona dawn and rubbed charcoal under my eyes in the theater dressing room. I pretended I had been at the hospital with you all night, pretended it was that night, not the night still to come, when I stood by your bed and waited for what we'd always known was coming. I pretended so that I could talk about it with my friends so I could hear them say *I'm sorry I'm sorry* so I could feel that someone heard what I was observing even if you wouldn't couldn't acknowledge it to me. And now that I have been in the hospital with my own potential cellular murderer—a cancer creeping through my colon so quietly that everything was fine everything was fine until it surprised me with its power its blood on my thighs its determination to consume me—now that I have been in the hospital I understand why you couldn't say *I am dying I am leaving you my wife my daughter I am dying I am disappearing and you will have lives I will never know.* I understand why you couldn't say that why it would break you why you talked to the cat in the dark.

I have always been a fiction writer. The lie that tells the truth my mantra my prayer my salvation born from witnessing over and over the truth being encased in the lie *everything is fine everything is fine everything is fine*. I will always tell you the truth, but you may have to unravel the narrative to find it.

My father had a heart transplant last night, I told my friend Greg as we hung out in the light booth after school for tech rehearsal on yet another show that kept me busy, kept me out of the house where you were stiffening up and dying, where everything was fine, where I saw periods in every encounter: this will be our last Christmas, our last birthday, our last drive together. But the periods I saw then were only commas. Until the electric hospital room. Until the machines flashing zeros crashing silent screams.

My best friend from North Carolina just committed suicide, I told my friend Jill when I cried during a sixth-period suicide prevention assembly. She held me against her big bones and I wanted to curl into her belly, be absorbed by her freckled flesh and disappear. *I don't know what I'll do without her. No one knew me like she did.* Jill just took it in, my best friend who had recently transferred in from Chicago, my friend who knew what it was like to leave a place behind, my friend.

Those were lies, but they were truth: *My father needs a new heart. My friend—my father—is dying and I don't know what I will do. No one sees me like he does.* The fiction let the truth come through so it wouldn't eat at my throat in the night.

I don't know if my friends believed me or not, but they pretended to. We were all pretending. We were on the edge of graduation, of leaving what had become familiar if not pleasant, pretending we knew what we were supposed to do next. We were slipping whiskey into Coke cans in chemistry class and assuming no one could tell. But why would we think anyone would notice? Everything was always fine.

9

It's 1949. I'm not alive yet, but from a branch in a pine tree in Wilmington, North Carolina, just far enough away to stay hidden, I'm watching them anyway: my father's family. I guess I am alive a little because my mother is living, soaring through fourth grade preparing to skip fifth, and though she's a thousand miles away in Brooklyn, New York, with her alcoholic mother and codependent father, she's carrying the egg that will one day ripen and meet my father's sperm and turn into me. I'm not sure which is most unlikely—that a single sperm can connect to a single egg and become a human or that two living humans can navigate the thousands of miles and billions of people to find each other. Both require absurd acts of faith and the mathematics of chance, yet they occur every day. They won't meet for fourteen years, and I won't have a name for twenty, but for now I'm looking out on Hewlett's Creek three miles west of the Atlantic Ocean.

My grandfather has just come in from the cornfield where he goes daily to escape from my grandmother. He's wearing work boots and blue pants. There's a floppy sunhat on his rectangular head—"that's the Cherokee"—my grandmother will one day say to me, not with pride but with disgust, her own family English and Scottish, traceable to the early days of colonization, proud Southern landholders immortalized in yellowed daguerreotypes in oval frames on dark stairwells. He squints when he looks into the sun. My grandmother's hair hasn't whitened yet and the edges of her lips haven't permanently twisted down. She's pulling the crab nets out of the creek; my aunt, a big girl now of nearly twelve, wrestles the snapping claws from the ropes and tosses them in the tin bucket. Neither of them wears a hat, though it's humid and the sun draws pulsing headaches from behind their eyes. I can't hear what they're saying, but the tone is friendly. My aunt's posture is ramrod straight. Even when she bends to remove the frantic crabs, she folds at right angles, gaze focused on her task.

The boy, who will become my father, is seven and he's running in circles with Wilbur, his brown and white pointer hound, trying to dry himself off from his dip in the creek. He kicks a red ball with his strong feet and Wilbur nudges it with his nose and the boy giggles and loves the way his bare toes leave indentions in the sandy ground. Freckles cluster on his cheeks; freckles I never saw during the years we were both embodied, and I want to reach down from the branch and touch them, but that's not allowed. Maybe the polio took the freckles as dessert after it ate the muscles of his leg. The freckles won't make it onto my own cheeks. My skin will be clear and pale, an extension of my mother's Finnish ancestry.

This will be his first defining day. His first knowledge that there is a "before." I look around over the steepled roof of the clapboard house, across the tops of elms and pines and oaks, to the other side of the creek where there's a sandbar filled with burrowing bugs and shells, but I can't find any trace of what is coming. I'm wondering if there's a vantage point where we can see the challenges that are about to happen to us, if there's any angle we can view our lives where we might intercept the trouble, but if there is, I'm in the wrong place. I see no bend in the tree line, hear no rumble beneath the earth, smell no hint of sulfur on the salty air. It's a Tuesday afternoon in the sticky summer and my father is just a boy running with his dog.

The boy trips and falls into a stunned silence followed by giggles when Wilbur laps his face. He stands back up, dusts his knees, and kicks the ball high to the sun, and for a split second I see a shadow lick its circumference, but it could be that I held a blink too long. Or it could be hindsight bias. I know what's coming so I claim to see its footprints, even in innocent shadows.

My grandfather catches the ball and in a rare moment of lightness, tosses it to the boy who has forgotten about the fall, forgotten about how easy it is to get back up on two strong legs. The boy jumps as high as he can, but Wilbur leaps higher and the ball is back in play, snout to big hands to small hands to snout in a circle that continues until the first firefly glows. I want to see something I never saw after I was born—my father carefree, running with abandon, unmarked by his first "before." I never saw his blue eyes unhaunted, and if I could, if I could get close enough right now to peer into them, how might I be different? If I am shaped by who he became then I must also be shaped by who he was before he became the man I knew. That boy running with his dog would have still been inside him, would have still been laughing even if many "afters" wrote different stories across that moment.

The crabs climb over each other, desperate to get out of the bucket, to get back to the creek, to slip into the murk, but my grandmother will have none of that and they go three-two-one into boiling water, the screams of the air releasing from their shells cutting through the dusk. The swamp frogs have begun singing, their calls like a drunkard blowing into a whiskey jug, a sound that imprints itself on me, forming the first layer on my forthcoming body. The inner core of my flesh, my earth.

My Home Layer.

It's August. The month I will be born, but for today the boy is laughing, hugging Wilbur and bounding up the stairs to wash his hands before supper. It's uneventful, as many meals are until you frame them through the lens of what comes next. Maybe the boy drinks milk, maybe juice. Maybe he winks an eye open during the prayer, just to see if anyone else is peeking. I don't notice because I am checking the chimney to make sure nothing could crawl down it in the night; I am locking the doors, skeleton keys turning snugly to the right beneath beveled crystal doorknobs; I am plugging the leak in the pipes to keep the rot from climbing up. I am everywhere and nowhere and even from my precarious perch I could see nothing, stop nothing.

There are no signs.

"Mother made ham that night," Dad-as-raven says, favoring his shorter leg. I startle. "Sorry. I hope you don't mind I let myself in your house."

My tuxedo cat BB hisses at the space he occupies, then runs away, ears flat. "Of course not." All I have ever wanted is to have him back in my house.

"The ham wasn't very good." His wing unfurls to reveal his pack of Pall Malls. "Do you mind?"

No. Yes. When I was little, I was terrified our house would burn down because he'd leave a cigarette on the windowsill, or he'd fall asleep with one still between his lips.

"Don't worry," he says. "This is all in your head anyway. Imagining isn't going to burn down anything."

Right.

"After I quit, I missed smoking every single day," he says. "Right up until the end, I could have eaten a pack whole."

I crack a window, just in case.

"I surely miss that dog."

I return to the boy, to the clapboard house, to the sandy earth and Wilbur. My aunt gathers the empty plates; grandfather prepares to wash them. It's his favorite thing. I remember he was in such a hurry to do the dishes he'd take our plates away from us mid-bite. But this night he is young, his back hasn't stooped and his voice hasn't disappeared, and my grandmother, in a blue cotton dress, is pretty, a swan's grace to her neck. I've never seen that. One afternoon, twelve years after I was born, we were in a fitting room together. She was trying on a shirt and I saw her huge heavy breasts falling to her belly button. I was horrified. Today, mine do the same.

The boy and his dog go into his bedroom and he changes into thin pajamas. The window is open, but there's no breeze. A black aluminum fan oscillates on his dresser, fluttering the edges of his Yankees baseball cards. Phil Rizzuto. Norman "Babe" Young. George Stirnweiss. And, of course, Babe Ruth. His wife-to-be is riding the subway with her father—the BMT line—Brooklyn-Manhattan Rapid Transit Corporation. She'll never get used to the new subway numbers, and when I travel with her many, many years from this day back to the City, she will point to every station and tell me what it used to be. She's a Dodgers fan. They used to be in Brooklyn.

The boy rubs at a swollen bite on his ankle. It's not possible to keep the mosquitoes out of the house.

"Make sure you say your prayers!" my grandmother shouts from the kitchen.

The boy folds to his knees, clasps his hands, and whispers memorized words. Does he believe then? I cannot tell from the sounds. I cannot tell from the folding of fingers and legs. He crawls into bed, lays on top of the sheet. It's too hot. Sweat pools at the base of his spine and begins to itch. His pajamas stick to his skin. A Frog FW-190 model airplane he built with his father hangs from a wire on the ceiling. The shadows from its wings stretch across the corner.

In just a few hours, the whole house is awakened by Wilbur's frantic barking behind the boy's closed door.

"Wilbur," the boy whispers. "Quiet down." But the words stick in his throat and he isn't sure if he spoke them or simply thought them. He'd been dreaming something huge and orange with a round face and thick legs. There'd been some music in his dreams. Loud trumpets maybe, or saxophones. Something brass and off-key. "Wilbur." His eyes are stuck together, like when he had pink eye. He can't feel his lower body. He must be twisted in his sheets. They are wrapped tight around his stomach, cutting off circulation to his feet and legs. He tries to catch the edges of his dream back. Sweat beads on his face, trickles down his flushed cheeks.

When he finally opens his eyes and sees moonlight falling across the crocheted coverlet, he is relieved he'll have a few more minutes to sleep. His mind is still heavy, so at first he thinks he is in the middle of that orange lucid dream and is unconcerned when he tries to roll to his right side and is unable to do his usual turn-around. He thinks his dizziness is part of the dream and doesn't worry right away. He doesn't notice he can't feel the usual morning coolness of the sheets or the pillow he likes to keep underneath his knees. He doesn't notice the headache, believing himself trapped in his dream, a prisoner of an evil villain. How is he going to escape? Who is coming to rescue him? He closes his eyes again. Maybe Doc Savage will leap down from the eighty-sixth floor of the Empire State Building like he does in the comics and save him from whatever trouble he's gotten into. He relaxes into that for a moment before the headache explodes into ice shards at the base of his skull, sending tickles of cool fire into his spine. His eyes reopen, hot and wet, and he is sure now that he is awake, that he cannot roll over in his pre-dawn bed, and that Doc Savage, even if he is on his way, can do nothing for him. An iron door closes inside him that he hadn't before realized existed. He has left his dream and entered a nightmare. "Mama," he says softly, his tongue thick and sticky. Something inside him slips the padlock on the iron door, a click, a spin, then silence.

Polio had come for the boy after all. He had known it was out there. The movie theater had been closed. The public pool. Even summer Bible school was cancelled, an action he was not opposed to since it freed up afternoons for sun and dogs and music. He had been upset about the movie theater the most, not wanting to miss whatever western would be the talk of school, but now it appears he isn't going to school. He isn't going to the movies or Bible school or baseball games, either. He isn't going to the beach or the river or his friends' houses or quail hunting with Wilbur. Instead, he is going to be quarantined.

He had dared it to come. He touched the girl with polio and went to the funeral of the boy who'd died. He thought he could outrun it. He'd been callous, hadn't prayed the prayers the pastor told him to, hadn't repented enough, though he wondered how many times and how many ways children were supposed to repent for being alive. A boy, no matter how fast he is, can't outrun what he can't see.

He is only partially aware of his mother screaming over his body, his dog spinning in circles on the rag rug, his sister chewing her fingernails in the corner of the room. The thin cold hand of his father slides under his head. He searches for the edges of his orange dream. If he stays in the dream, the polio will pass through him and he will wake up in the sun with the radio in the background whispering him alive.

The Raven is silent. He has tried to eat his pack of Pall Malls and the cellophane threads have wrapped around his beak. It's fitting he doesn't speak. He never told me anything about that day, never spoke about the years he couldn't walk. I knew of the polio through newspaper clippings. He was a March of Dimes poster child for a time, his thin frame clad in only underwear, his withered leg hanging, hands gripped around two bars as he held himself up. A nurse in stiff white smiled next to him. *Help him walk again. Every dime matters.* I knew of it from the rise in one shoe and the limp that made him fall down the driveway on the way to get the paper in the morning, from the way he'd learned to use his hand to lift and cross his leg when seated, and from the times he had me walk across his back before I got too heavy to ease the knots.

Aside from a few emotional scars, I beat the polio. Yes, Dad, but those scars inked my own body. I'm left to conjure them now so I can find the way they've rooted in me and unravel your scars from mine. I wanted so much for you not to die that I took everything of yours I could, whether you meant me to have it or not. It's not all the parents' doing. Children are greedy. We take everything.

Raven

Your mother she is practical and patient and persistent and she will persevere with silent grace and maybe one day you will know her as I know her for she is like no other no other she saw me saved me saw me. She never thought I was broken when my whole family called me sinner called me weak called me guilty of the shame of illness of displeasing God of being unworthy of love, but she quieted those voices in me with her silent steadfast stance her cool hand on my attacked heart her smile wide as the Cape Fear River.

But you, daughter, have always attached, held tight to roots in red clay, fought tooth and claw to avoid change. You hold until the things you grasp dissolve. You will never be the one to turn away to say goodbye first to walk out the door you chose to enter, and this will be your power and your struggle. I see you now anchoring yourself to the hospital room floors—mine where I died and yours thirty years later where they cut out from your belly what you were no longer capable of releasing. Your feet grow suction cups that stick to linoleum and your ankles swell with sadness you refuse to shake away because to have no sadness means to have no center and if you have no center you will fall apart.

But I have fallen apart now and the center still holds.

I see from sea to sea and also from then to there. This moment is a chapter unscrolling from before I was born until long after you have joined me here in this place of one long continuous breath. The shock. The light. The sounds. Here there is no sound. Except maybe—wait, hear ye hear ye who goes there?

Raven's Father

It wasn't like you think it was. Not either of you. I wanted to do so much more than I did. So much more than I could have.

You don't remember what it was like when you got polio, and, granddaughter, you don't know at all what we went through and what we did. Son, I would have given my legs to you, my heart. I would have given it all. When I met your mother, I thought she was the most beautiful woman I'd ever seen. She was seductive and sensual and smart and I was just a farm kid. We grew things, my family, for hundreds of years. My land—the land that should have been yours—the land that your daughter sold when Mother died—was our land since 1735.

Me

I didn't want to sell it. I couldn't afford to keep it.

Raven

Home! Home! Home by the creek by the sea by the sea I see.

Raven's Father

I see you both going back to the land—the pretty place by the creek, the creek that just flooded again in the hurricane, the creek that swells with alligators and crabs and skate bugs. The creek that we thought might have given you polio. That creek, it flows in your blood because it is ours, the creek.

It was hard to have you leave, son. It was hard when your new wife took you from us, took you to a big city, then took you away to the West. I didn't want to hold you back, but you'll never know how much I held.

We waited for your letters like food. Your words of the weather, of your golf, your health; they were the bridge that was left between your mother and me. They were the things we held on to, they were what she saved. Laraine has your words now. She's trying once again to write the book about you and her and your words help.

There's the letter from your hospital bed in 1976 after your heart attack when your printing looked like a kindergartener's. The one three days before you died when you wrote about being exhausted, wondering why the polio was creeping back, wondering why your heart was not as strong as your spirit. And then I came to you in a dream, three days before you died, and you thought it was an omen for my death. You were so undone by it—me in our field, on our land, in my straw hat with my blue eyes that were lights instead of shadows—you thought I was leaving you, but, son, I never left you. You started to write my eulogy and your wife saved it all these decades and gave the scrap of envelope to my granddaughter after her cancer arrived.

He was a man of a simpler time. A man of simple needs, great patience, and enduring commitments. He was my father.

So undone were you by that dream you stepped into the in-between and went ahead of me. You told your wife, "My father is dying," and at the same time your daughter told her friend, "My father is dying," and both of you were right.

When you died, I shrunk, not inches but feet, and when my granddaughter came to visit us two years after, she was taller than me. Still, we could not talk because we had never talked because we were from a different time and she had been taken from us to the West. Your mother, son, she took up whiskey, and I went out to the barn where we used to go together to talk, where we had to put down that old hunting dog, and I wept so hard I thought I'd ruin my soil with the salt. I did this every day until my own heart died. I don't know that we knew how to love, your mother and I, and our own love, well, it wasn't what I'd hoped, but we held that bridge of you between us.

You were our placeholder.

I should have written more. I should have called. But it doesn't matter now. What matters is that the stories get told straight. I need to make sure that you know, son, that Laraine knows, that I never thought you were less than perfect. I need you to know that if you look behind you, here in the wherever we are, you'll see me. You'll know me by my straw hat. I've been waiting since before you were born.

10

I untangle the cellophane and his beak snaps open. "Why do you think my leg is still lame?" he asks. "All those scars went with me. Turns out there are some things you do take with you when you die."

"I'm not looking to blame anybody," I say, and it is truth. A parent can't escape imprinting his children. I'm curious. I want to understand what I wasn't able to see when he was alive. I want to see what I couldn't ask about because when I learned of my cancer, something uncorked in me. I have to change everything. I'm not looking for a problem. I'm trying to pre-empt future ones by figuring out what got me here. I need to make a list. A plan. What else, besides cancer, have I not seen that is waiting for its perfect moment to strike?

Okay, Dad, I've got another possible answer to the riddle. They don't tell you that illness will reset your time clock. Where once you saw infinite space to wander, you now see your expiration date. True, you don't know the actual time, but you know you won't be the one who lives forever. You don't realize you carried that magical thinking with you into middle age until illness cuts its hubris off at the knees.

"Sometimes," he says, deadpan. "Illness just cuts off your knees."

"Tell me about the years you were in the hospital with polio," I say. He turns away. "Tell me because I was so afraid you'd die my whole life that I think I did everything I could to hold on to every scrap of paper, every conversation, every fight, so that when you did die I could rebuild you and keep you safe forever. I kept more of you than I should and I need different stories and I can't ask you because you're gone."

He laughs, a croak-caw. "I'm *gone*?" His wings stretch.

"I'm imagining you, right?"

"What else is there but imagination?"

"I have to feed Barnessa."

"Oh, Sugar," and there it is, the disappointment. "You named the damn cat."

I have to go feed my barn cat before it gets dark. If anything happens to her, I will break. She chose me. She arrived a week after I returned home from the hospital. Her ribs poked through her skin, her belly sunk. She'd run when I put food out and the day, months later, when she let me pet her head while she ate, I cried.

We had cats growing up. With names. Charley. Beezus. Tiger. But to him, a dog person, they were always "the damn cat." The year he died, I came home from school early and caught him on the patio talking to Beezus. I watched from the kitchen window and when he finished the conversation, I pretended like I'd just arrived. I wish I'd asked what they had talked about. "Barnessa McBarncat."

"Well then, go tend to her."

I don't know if I should leave him alone in the house, but I need to feed the cat before the sun goes down. The coyotes and owls hunt best at twilight.

"Go on, feed the damn cat."

"How do I know you'll be here when I come back?"

"Are you ready to let me leave?"

We both know the answer to that, so I nod and go out to the patio. Barnessa is waiting, curled in a flowerpot under the alligator juniper tree. She trills hello and runs to me. Another day. She's here with me one more day.

Raven's Mother

They were coming to take me to the home the day after the evening I died. I went with your sister the day of my death to see the place and she tried to tell me how nice it was and how I would be so much happier there and all kinda nonsense. It was fancy, to be sure, all dark mahogany and doilied furniture, creaky wood floors that reminded me of my daddy's house back in the day. I'd told that girl, your big sister, and I'da told you if you hadn't gone up and died on us all the way across the country, I won't never go into no home. It astonishes me that after all the years I been her mama she forgot how determined I am, how when I say I ain't or I is then I ain't or I is. I never say I ain't and then turn to an is. Folks say I was complicated but I wasn't complicated at all. I was just a woman who knew her own mind and nobody knew right what to do with me. Your sister, she paid a lot for that fancy home where I wasn't never going to lay me down and I let her pay, knowing that big fancy deposit she was go'n to lose was her own fault for not believing her mama when she say what she's go'n do or not do. Mother always knows best.

The room she was fixing to put me in had a big picture window what looked out on a garden filled up with yellow roses and azalea. Was supposed to be some kind of peaceful, but an old folks' home ain't nothing but an above ground coffin. If I'm go'n in a coffin, then I'm go'n in the ground like the good Lord intended. Anything else is disrespecting the natural order.

Besides which, I had a home. Our home. Your home. Your daddy's home. He built that home, literally with his own hands. That home stood us through three hurricanes, but somehow your sister thought that home wasn't good enough for me anymore. Like you thought that home wasn't good enough for you anymore. Son, I don't know how you could forget what it was, what we did for you, what it meant to be ours.

I recollect she figured I wasn't fit to be living on my own what because she saw me talking to the air, but I wasn't talking to no air. I had all my senses. I was talking to you and to your daddy up *in* the air, both of you hanging around pestering me like horseflies, but I'll give you it was good to visit.

Boy, I done told you all of your life, this here's your home. Don't know why you were so surprised to find yourself back here when you crossed.

Home, child, is a commitment.

11

You're in your mother's house in Scottsdale. This is not the house you lived in with your father. It is not a house that has held you. Still, it's a mile from the hospital and that's convenient. Gratitude is riding on fear waves when you wake at 3:30, shower with antibacterial soap, and perform sun salutations in a dark bedroom, running your hands over your yet-to-be-sliced belly telling her *I love you I love you I love you.*

Then.

You're separated from your family at 5:30 a.m. and taken with a group of six down a wood-paneled hallway into an older, darker portion of the hospital. You're assigned a bed and given a plastic bag for your clothes. You have to take your third pregnancy test in three days because, why the eff not, even though you haven't had anything to eat and very little but Gatorade mixed with Miralax in three days in preparation for your second colonoscopy in two weeks and the major surgery, and besides, you haven't felt very sexy since the rectal bleeding began six months ago in October.

You tell them your name, again, confirm your birthday, again, and they scan your barcode on your ID bracelet, which is next to a wristband that contains the numbers for your blood vials, which are stored somewhere in this building should you need a blood transfusion, permission for which you had to give forty-eight hours previously. Your allergies are marked on a red band, and now you have three bracelets.

Judy, the ostomy nurse, comes in and you like her, but you're afraid of her because she means you might have to have a colostomy bag. She tells you your belly is perfect for a bag as she puts two blue dots where it would go, and since it is perfect, you won't need one. But you know she must say that to all the bellies, all the days, before all the surgeries. Still, you like her and very few people have said your belly was perfect. The anesthesiologist comes in and you again confirm your name and date of birth and she scans your barcode and tries to assure you that she—that they all—have done this before. She tells you what they will be giving you, how they will be monitoring you, but you do not have a medical degree and you have no idea what she is saying.

Your surgeon comes in after you're hooked up with your IV and your various other medicines that you don't understand but you put in your mouth anyway because those are the rules. Your feet are strapped in compression socks and held to the bed in automatic compression sleeves, which squeeze your calves every sixty seconds. They are tethers to the bed. Tethers to the earth. You hate anything on your toes, but you don't want a blood clot, and they don't appear optional, and you most definitely want the tumor out—you've already paid for it—so you don't say anything. Your toes will just have to adjust.

They said you would be slightly upside down, with a ventilator tube, so that the belly would be most exposed, most available to Eva, the room-sized floor-to-ceiling robot that will be performing the surgery. You don't remember the ventilator tube, but you felt the rawness on the roof of your mouth like you were told you would. You have never worn a bikini or a belly shirt, but now everything depends on your opening up your most yin side—your most vulnerable parts, belly up—to fluorescent lights and strangers in masks and gloves. And you have to open. You have to welcome in the robot so that your body won't be afraid. So that when this is over and Eva is done, your body will grasp itself with love and rebuild its muscles because it knows that you're in this together—for the long game. Your beautiful, beautiful body.

Whatever they give you upon leaving pre-op kicks in before reaching the operating room and you never actually see the room or the floor-to-ceiling robot named Eva who will be doing the cutting and the sewing and the biopsying. You are glad her name is Eva and you are glad that you are with people who would name a robot and you are sure your surgeon has done this before and all will be well. But you don't think any of that in the operating room because you don't have any awareness there.

But your body does.

You wake up in post-op. First thought: You are not dead. Second thought: Is there a bag? Your hand goes to your belly and feels only flesh. Your body is wracked with pain from the gas they blew into your belly so Eva had room to work. There is nowhere for it to go. It has to take its time. You have to wait it out. You've felt very little physical pain in your life, and it is strange that the body takes its own way without your mind to stop it or control it. You can't roll over because of the compression socks and there's a strange tightness in your belly, as if it didn't really believe it was going to be cut open, or that if it was, the flesh wouldn't remember.

You watch your body contract and expand, trying to shift on the tiny bed, which has your feet held prisoner in the ever-compressing compression sleeves and you have a moment of clarity in which you realize that you are calm, even as your body screeches. You float inside of it. You are not your body.

You're hot, so they bring you ice. You're cold, so they take it away. Someone wipes your mouth with a swab because you're so thirsty but you can't drink anything yet. You're a horse, baring her teeth for a brush. You press your morphine button because you can. You don't really see anyone's faces. Only their hands.

You wait in post-op for six hours until a room is ready. You are regaining some lucidity and are ready for a different gown. A shower. A fucking cheeseburger. But there's none of that. Just sweat and hair is matted to your head. But there is no co-lostomy bag, only a catheter and a urine bag, but that is okay.

You are alive.

They take you up to your room and just like in the movies, six pairs of hands, three on each side, lift you on your sweaty sheet onto the new bed. They roll you onto one side and pull the sheet out. They roll you onto the other and straighten a new one. Your room has two windows and a bathroom, but you remain tethered to the bed with compression sleeves, a catheter, and an IV drip for food and a morphine drip for sanity. You want to eat. You want to sleep. You want to roll into a ball. You want to storm the castle and say hell, yes, I am here. But all you can do is hit the morphine button, which doesn't do much except make things fuzzy. You don't like it. The pain is less, so you start to wean yourself off the morphine and on post-op day two, they take it away, along with the catheter and the urine bag and the IV feeding tube. You remove the compression sleeves because you hate them and you hide your feet under the bed when the nurses come in. You massage your legs yourself and walk around the hospital on your own. You are over it.

You get to move from clear liquids to full liquids, which is essentially ice cream, which is not really that good for you, and you feel that you have too much sugar too fast. It's been five days since you have had solid food. The next day, you get to move to a low-residue diet, which is mostly bananas, white bread, eggs, processed pastas, and clear liquids. You want your resection to stay together, so you buy foods you've moved away from over the years as you've pushed toward eating more healthfully. You've already lost fifteen pounds since the first colonoscopy. Maybe you'll write that weight-loss guide after all and finally get to meet Oprah.

You have to hold your IV hand outside the shower door because they left the tubing in your hand just in case, but still you take a one-armed shower all by yourself and you are the fucking bomb. You brush your teeth in a sink, not a plastic tub. The nurses offer either Oxycodone or Tylenol and you laugh. Is there nothing in the middle? But there isn't, so you take two Tylenol at 350 mg each and call it a night. You use your Raven and Thieves aromatherapy oils from your massage therapist and put chakra balancing music on your iPad. You hold your belly in your hands and tell her she is the most beautiful thing. That your whole body is the strongest, most beautiful thing.

The next morning you want some more Tylenol and the nurse says you're only allowed one Tylenol now and you laugh and tell her you can walk across the street to CVS and buy Tylenol in 500 mg tablets and take ten of them, and just last night they were offering Oxycodone. You call them fickle and everyone laughs. You like your nurses. They like you. You are not interested in staying here or being identified with your surgery. You are interested in rebuilding.

You talk to them and make jokes and they start to tell you about their lives and you sit in the hall together and look at the photographs. One of them talks about her own cancer scare. Another about the death of her daughter, and you just sit together on the bench, a picture of Bryce Canyon in front of you. You miss them when you leave.

You walk out four days later. No Tylenol. No prescriptions. Five robot kisses on your belly, a large incision above the pubic bone, and two perineum incisions. As you prepare to leave room 2611, you give thanks to it for holding you in the dark, for all the machines that beeped and compressed and fed and drained you. You write a thank you note to the nurses of post-surgical oncology, and a note to your surgeon. Your tumor is gone. There is no cancer in the lymph nodes. You are the luckiest woman on the planet, but not because the outcome was so good. You are the luckiest woman on the planet because you felt, especially in post-op, that no matter what is happening, all is well. You felt the eternal part of you—the part that one day will be stardust—and you now know in your body what you have observed as you've watched the illnesses and deaths of others.

You are not alone. Everywhere there are hands whose job it is to hold you, and when the moment is perfect, to set you free.

Full stop.

I want to believe this because it's the ending everyone wants to read. Maybe it is the truth, but I've skipped ahead like always, wanting the illumination without the darkness. Leapfrogging over the feelings that scare me because everything is fine.

Bypassing the emotions doesn't mean they cease to exist. They just move underground and strengthen.

My father agrees, as evident by the cawing-laughing raven. "That's pretty," says Dad-as-raven, fanning his feathers. "Tied up rather neatly, don't you think? You told everyone what they wanted to hear at the end."

I bristle. People liked that piece. *The Manifest-Station* published it. I regress to academics. "I made an arc. There's supposed to be a transformation."

"Yes," he says. "But you skipped over the skinning. You couldn't even claim the *I.*"

I look back at the piece. The last few paragraphs wrapped it up. Made meaning out of the experience. Made me brave and strong and powerful. They constructed me into the image I wanted to share. But I know what he means. I wrote the truth that tells the lie.

"All right," Dad-as-raven says. "I'll give you one of the answers to the question of what they don't tell you. They don't tell you what it's like in your mind at three in the morning. Can you write the night? And can you do it in first person or do you have to keep the barrier up even on the page?"

I need to shimmy sideways into that, so please allow my best coping strategy and defense mechanism to emerge: enter Academic Voice.

❦

Epigenetics: The study of heritable changes in gene function that do not involve changes to the DNA sequence. Scientific studies on nematode worms and mice and tomato plants are revealing to scientists that experiences from previous generations can be passed on to future generations. In *Requiem for a Nun,* William Faulkner wrote, "The past is never dead. It's not even past." Now, the scientific doorway is being opened to the possibility that humans can inherit memories of their ancestors' experiences over as many as fourteen generations. It's complicated, and I'm no geneticist, but I am a storyteller, and we writers have long known that our ancestors' lives shape our own, regardless of whether we directly heard their stories. What's been the stuff of shamanism and sorcery is gaining ground in empirical data, but until then, the imagination takes hold and the storyteller travels backward, black-and-white photos in hand, to make sense out of who she grew into, to till the soil of the dead until the spirits stop rising and can start to rest.

Please listen: I am trying to tell you something true about grief and attachment and the shape-shifter that is home, but I am failing because I can't look straight at it, so first I'm going to tell you a story about my father because his stories merged with my mother's stories and I inherited much more than green eyes and a ski-jump nose and a love of books. And today, when I find myself standing between two lives, I have nowhere to look for understanding but the past, which does not die, but reinvents itself, masquerading as new thoughts, laughing at our feeble attempts to quiet its fury. One thing is certain: the past cannot be locked in a trunk. Its messages will tattoo themselves on your skin, and the secret decoder ring is story.

A 5-Minute Play Interlude

CUE: Transitional music

INT: Therapist 1's office. It's sunny, mid-afternoon. 1990. I am twenty-two, and it is three years after Dad died.

ME

_____.

THERAPIST 1

_____.

ME

_____.

THERAPIST 1
(twirls expensive pen between her fingers)
ME

_____.

THERAPIST 1
(looks at expensive watch)
ME

_____.

THERAPIST 1

I'm afraid our time is up.

-End-

CUE: Transitional music

INT: Therapist 2's office. It's sunny, mid-afternoon. 1997. I am twenty-nine, and it is ten years after Dad died.

                                ME

_____.

                          THERAPIST 2

Can you elaborate on that?

                                ME

I don't think so.

                          THERAPIST 2

Mmmm.

                                ME

I feel like I'm whining.

                          THERAPIST 2

That's interesting. What do you mean by whining?

                                ME

Like I'm telling the same story over and over again and can't
get past it.

                          THERAPIST 2

(scribbles notes on legal paper) Mmmm.

                                ME

Mmmm what?

                          THERAPIST 2

(scribbles notes on legal paper) Interesting.

                                ME

Fuck this.

                          THERAPIST 2

(scribbles notes on legal paper) Interesting.

                                ME

What are you writing?

                          THERAPIST 2

Just notes.

ME

Show me.

THERAPIST 2

That wouldn't be a good idea.

ME

Why not? It's about me.

THERAPIST 2

Yes, but, it's not generally a good idea for the client to see these notes.

ME

Why?

THERAPIST 2

You might misconstrue—

ME

What? My own life?

THERAPIST 2

(scribbles intently)

- End-

I never saw the notes. Here's what I believed was there:

Possible Schizotypal Personality Disorder 301.22 (F21) - reduced capacity for close relationships; magical thinking; unspecified hallucinations; cognitive distortions - pt believes she is speaking to her dead father in the form of a raven. Seeks guidance from hallucination. Experiences sensory engagement with hallucination (smoke from cigarettes). Pt understands father is deceased yet is unable to enter new reality without attachment figure.

Possible Adult Separation Attachment Anxiety Disorder 309.21 (F93.0) - bereavement complications?

Possible Post-Traumatic Stress Disorder 309.81 (F43.10) - with depersonalization? Pt witnessed death of father; not traumatic death, long-term illness, but pt stuck in ~~avoidance~~ immersive tactics to remain in a co-dependent relationship with the deceased. Vivid dreams reinforce this illusion.

Persistent Complex Bereavement Disorder. (No diagnostic code. Area for further study) 10 years since father's death. Preoccupation with circumstances of death. Revisits day of death. Pt alone in hospital room with father when he died. Bitterness/anger related to loss, stemming from guilt. Difficulty trusting other individuals since the death. Diminished sense of identity (feeling that a part of herself died with the deceased).

12

Confess your sins and you shall be healed.

If this boy is to do your work, Lord, please spare him. If not, please spare another.

God is testing you.

How have you displeased God so he visited this illness upon you?

If you were truly a good person, God would not have made you sick.

How have you sinned, boy? Fall on your knees before Him so that you might be healed of this affliction.

Dad grew up in a fundamentalist home in the heart of Southern Baptist country. In the evangelical brain seasoned with the spice of prosperity gospel madness, illness was a direct result of actions or inactions. Rewards, such as wealth, health, and beauty, were divinely bestowed to the worthy. For that cluster of illogic to hold, illness, poverty, and physical afflictions must be punishments from that same God. For that tumor of misbeliefs to thrive, it must consume the life around it.

Dad didn't hear those phrases only as a child, but every living day of his life. The doubts clawed at him when his heart failed thirty years after polio ate his leg. He was a sinner. Born a sinner. Struggled through life as a sinner, and I have no idea how he felt at the end of his life when his heart said "no more." Did he still see himself as fallen? Or could he see the marvel that he was, that all of us are? Was he still afraid of some mythical fire pit of damnation? Or was he just ready to be done with it all?

"It sure follows you around, that voice," Dad-as-raven says.

It follows me around too, even though those words were rarely spoken directly to me. Even though my father tried to shield me from them. He couldn't protect me from himself, and so he also couldn't avoid exposing me to the stories that wrapped their arms around him. We all lived together in our house. My parents, their stories, and me.

"So, were they right?" I ask.

He goes mute. I'm hoping that because he's here talking to me, albeit as a raven, that even if he's in that promised hell pit, it must be lax enough to allow him out from time to time.

"What if," he says, "it doesn't matter if they were or weren't right? What if none of the stories matter at all?"

They have to matter. Stories are how we make sense of the world. They're how we give our lives context.

"That's the thing," he says, reading my thoughts. "They give your life context. But that's all they are. The context, not the life."

When he was alive, he said things like this, especially towards the end. He'd known that he was unlikely to see old age. He sped time up, and by his death at forty-six, he was stooped and gray, easily mistaken for someone twenty years older. I'm always surprised by that when I see the last pictures I have of him. In my mind, his hair is still black, his skin still pink with youth. Which is the true story? Which is Dad? The one in my memory? The one in the photo? The one who's shapeshifted into a raven, blowing smoke rings at me on my porch?

> Dear Daddy,
> I need to know how you lived with the knowledge that your body was turning on you. In the middle of the night when I wake up, still feeling the pinch of the oxygen tube in my nose, I wonder if there is one cell in my body turning itself off, going rogue, preparing to write a story of malignancy. Did you always wonder when the next heart attack would come? When the polio virus would wake up again?
> Love,
> Me

Cancer cells are fundamentalists, living at the expense of the other cells in the body. They are willing to kill their host to survive, just like my father's family was willing to sacrifice his life to satisfy their hungry God.

When I was diagnosed, many well-meaning friends told

me to "kick cancer's ass." That couldn't be farther from my intention. I appreciated their hopes for my well-being, and I definitely wanted to live, but I immediately altered their words in my mind. I didn't want to put cancer on high alert. I didn't want it to be preparing for a battle with me—an opponent unskilled at war. A cancer cell is not an invader. It's not a virus we contracted or a bacterial infection. It is our own cells. It is us, going off-book, acting against our own best interests.

The primary Western medical methods of cancer treatment focus on dominance, elimination, and extermination, and those are the *same methods* the cancer cell uses. It understands those stories. It *lives* those stories.

For a cancer cell to change, it must learn a new expression of its DNA. For a father to become a raven, he must embrace a new form. For a daughter to understand her own cancer and her own grief, she must learn a new way to write.

∽

"The findings are consistent with Lynch Syndrome," says Dr. Zieve, pausing to give me time to process these words that I didn't understand. When I don't respond, he tries again. "Do you have questions?"

It has been only a few weeks since I put on the blue cotton backless gown and voluntarily surrendered my bowels to the giant robot named Eva who meticulously removed a foot of my colon and sewed the new ends back together. "Like a garden hose," my surgeon, Dr. Kassir, had said, making a motion with his hands which indicated this resection was as simple as snapping back two Legos into place.

Any questions?

Dr. Zieve is an integrative physician—a Western-trained medical doctor who'd jumped ship in the nineties after years of frustration with a system focused not on patients but on pharmaceuticals. He now focuses exclusively on cancer care. He wears too-round eighties-style glasses and his ruffled hair lends him the stereotypical mad-scientist look. We'd run a comprehensive genetic test on my tumor and the seven-page report consisted of columns of letters that indicated gene sequences. He circles four genes. "Here. See they're mutated? That's consistent with Lynch. We can only know conclusively with a blood test." He waits again, politely.

In the last month, I'd dealt with more doctors than in the previous forty years. Most of them didn't wait for anything; they barreled forward, assured of their decision, comfortable with another box to check off on the standardized pre-authorized treatment plan. They did not leave space for questions. They did not deviate from protocol, from best practices. They viewed every patient as a number and a data point. I have spent my life hiding and now I desperately need to be seen.

Cancer is its own country with its own laws and treatises and terms. Though I knew I'd have to struggle with its language, I hadn't expected to have to keep repeating my name to its administration. I hadn't expected at every consultation to re-declare my sovereignty, to establish my own boundaries, to push back against the robotic: *Drink this. Eat this.* One pill makes you larger. One pill makes you small. Fuck you. I refused all the pills and ran from this cancer-country run by white coats and insurance companies and underwritten with the language of war.

Even as I ran, brambles scratching at my bare legs, the skin on my back open to the sky, blue cotton gown falling off my shoulders, I heard the voices:

She's read too many books. She's questioning too much. Why can't you just for once do what people say? You don't know everything. Pride goeth before a fall. What, now you think you're a medical doctor? You don't know what's best for you. Look, here's the chart. This is your tumor. This is your life expectancy. These are your odds. Drink this. Eat this. Why are you running? Why is she running? Don't you know we're trying to save your life?

The doctors' coats are embroidered with the names of their pharmaceutical overseers. The prescription pads marked with logos, allegiances. *Don't leave the country,* they shout at me as I run and run and run and run, crossing the border into the dark. *We can't help you over there,* they shout. *You're responsible for what happens now! You signed a waiver. Didn't she sign the waiver?* The white coats nod to each other. *Yes, yes, look, here's her signature.* Relieved, they click their emblazoned pens and write me off, non-compliant, another casualty of the war.

"What does that mean?" I say to Dr. Zieve when the silence is too much for even me, an introvert addicted to quiet. My belly is still purple and blue. Eva's meticulousness had not been without carnage. My escape through the forest dark over the beeping border of machines designed to tether me to the institution's central hub had not been without sacrifice.

"Oh, of course." He springs into teacher-mode. "Lynch Syndrome is an inherited genetic condition that indicates increased risk in a variety of cancers, especially colon cancer, but there's also elevated risk for endometrial cancers, breast cancers, liver, lung, and skin cancer." He winds down his recitation, crossing his hands on his desk. "Any questions?"

You can still come back to us, the cancer-country proclaims in its cocky victorious cackle. *We'll be here. We're always here. Drink this. Eat this. Let us help you. You, silly girl, precious young thing, you thought you knew better. Silly girl. We're waiting.*

I take a breath into my ripped-open belly. Yes. I have one question, but it isn't for him. It is for me. What will I do with this inheritance? This typo in my genetic code? This misfiring of a sequence?

In Lynch Syndrome, at least one of five key genes—MLH1, MSH2, MSH6, PMS2, or EPCAM contains an alteration that can prevent the cellular repair of a cancer cell. In my inheritance, four out of five of those genes contains the mutation. Yay! Four of a kind. A pretty decent hand in Texas Hold'em. But not *so clear* of a hand that you'd not have decisions to make about your next moves at the table.

The scientific definition of *inherit* is simple: The acquisition of traits genetically transmitted from parent to offspring. That sounds very, well, scientific. Very black and white. Very *permanent*. It sounds like the story *has been written*. Note the passive voice in the preceding sentence. The genetic expression has been written by someone other than me. This hand of cards—this chapter—that appears in my timeline seems to have a fixed outcome. But ask any poker player—any hand can be a winner and any hand can be a loser. And if you asked Kenny Rogers, he'd say, "The best that you can hope for is to die in your sleep."

Subplot: I also inherited my father's love of old country music.

The verb inherit comes from the Latin *inhereditare*: to appoint as heir. As the word's story progressed to Middle English, it mutated and became *enherite*: to receive as a right. *To receive* has a different connotation than *transmit*. *To receive* implies reception—a willingness to accept this gift. This right. This inheritance.

If I am willing to accept Lynch Syndrome, part of my inheritance, as a gift, then how does that change the structure of the narrative?

If I have inherited mismatched protein repair genes, have I also inherited mismatched illness stories?

How have I sinned?

What must I confess?

How can I be loved if I've been marked by illness?

Where is the author of all of these stories? I think it's time we had a little chat.

"You'll never get an appointment," says Dad-as-raven. "The schedule is always full."

"I'm not asking for an appointment," I say. "I'm just going to show up and take back the pen. I accept the inheritance. I do not accept the predetermined end."

Dad-as-raven lights his cigarette, the blue smoke rings wrapping around my fingers like jewels. I think I hear a chuckle from the center of his beak, but it might just be my own wish for him to still be talking, my own hope that his story also hasn't ended.

Raven

I inherited old time religion and a God of fear and a malformed heart.

Raven's Father

I inherited the land that we had stolen four hundred years ago from the Tuscarora Indians when the first Herring made his way from Scotland, but we never talked about that.

Raven's Mother

I inherited fear of poverty and fear of shame and fear of God. I inherited racism and I passed that on to you. I inherited a need to control and a judgment of myself that I turned on everyone.

Me

I inherited hoarding from my grandmother; a love of sand and sea from my grandfather; colon cancer from my father; everything is fine from my mother. I inherited a slaveholding past and a will to live from everyone.

Raven

Inheritance is more than DNA and bones. Inheritance is patterns trauma loans of sadness anger fear that build up strength inside a body and travel down the family tree from you to you to me to me and, daughter, pay attention here you can reweave the fabric of your flesh but you must take each piece apart and bless it cut it return it to the earth and do not pass it on. Gift the world only what is useful.

13

When I would get birthday money and Christmas money as a girl, I never spent it. I accumulated the one- and five-dollar bills—the occasional amazing ten-dollar bill—and rolled them tight with a rubber band. I liked the unusual thickness of the paper, the shade of green, maybe I even liked the idea that money was a metaphor. What better for a writer than to hold a piece of paper that was a symbol for something else? It wasn't just that a five-dollar bill meant five one-dollar bills or twenty quarters. A five-dollar bill meant a stuffed animal, or a set of calligraphy pens, or three books at the Scholastic Book Fair. Having money in your pocket meant you could say no to things you didn't want to do. You could say no to people you didn't want to hang out with. You could travel wherever you wanted to. Money was more than power. Money was autonomy.

That bicentennial summer when you had your heart attack, I was slipping another five-dollar bill I'd gotten for my birthday into my roll when my mother saw me holding my stack of small-billed savings. "Where did you get all that?" she asked.

"Birthday money," I said. "Christmas money."

Suddenly, I felt like I was holding something dead and pungent. I didn't know—how could I at three days past eight years old—how much things cost in the adult world. I didn't understand that your heart attack caused you to leave work, which made it so no money was coming in. I didn't understand that my brilliant mathematician mother had given up her job to stay home for a few years while I was young, which meant that when your income dried up, all money dried up. I didn't understand that the piles of coupons Mom was always cutting and stacking and clipping together were also metaphors. I didn't understand how very sick you were. I didn't know that the doctors had already told you you wouldn't live out the year and that you'd told them to fuck off. I didn't know the edge we were teetering on because my mother, who was staring open-mouthed at my gift money, had ensured I believed everything was fine.

"How much do you have?" she said at last.

I didn't know, so I counted. "One hundred and ten dollars." A fortune in ones and fives. Two tens. I didn't know how much of a fortune. A car payment. A power bill. Gasoline. Food.

"What are you saving it for?" This question, and the sharpness of her tone, surprised me. Everything I'd been taught about money up until then was about saving it—for a rainy day, for something special, for an unanticipated problem. How could you both spend it and save it?

I didn't know what I was saving it for. A rainy day. Something special. An unanticipated problem. *Autonomy.*

"You better start spending some of it," she said. "You don't want to end up like Grandmama."

Another puzzling statement. Your mother was no one's favorite—her aggrieved Lost Cause of the South melodrama, her insistence on being called *Mother*, her single strand of pearls and blood-red lips—but I didn't understand how my small-bill roll was anything like her at all. I didn't want to be like her; none of us did. Mom left me there in my room, and the pride I'd felt at saving so much money over so many years of birthdays had turned to tar. The weight of the bill roll, once a solid root, grew teeth. The money would devour me and turn me into your mother. It would make me mean.

I didn't know my own mother, with her master's degree in mathematics, had just taken a job delivering the afternoon *Pennysaver* newspaper to the block twice a week. I didn't know how much it cost to be in the critical care ward for four weeks, how quickly money evaporates when there's no resupply, how money meant food. Medicine. Walls.

I also didn't know that she had just asked your mother to borrow a small stack of bills, just a little thicker than mine, to pay the mortgage. To buy pasta and bread and milk. To take care of me. I didn't know your mother had said no, they didn't have any to spare, they were stretched thin too, they were sorry but they couldn't help. I didn't know how wealthy she was, her house the same clapboard house you grew up in, the same bare bulbs dangling from fixtures, the same thin gray carpet, but my mother knew. Yet when my Southern grandmother died, nine years after you did, and left an estate worth almost a million dollars divided between your sister and me, when the inheritance check arrived—the check that allowed me to earn not one but two graduate degrees, buy a home, take a risk and relocate to a tiny mountain town, travel, save for retirement, and pay for my own hospital stay when cancer visited me—a smaller check, a check for $25,000 was included for my mother. "You were a good wife to Glenn," my grandmother said, and my mother, still working, still saving, still supporting, held that check for almost a year. She couldn't deposit it. She couldn't use it. *Blood money*, she said. How could we spend this money? This money that should have helped you when you were alive. This money that your mother would not share when it would have mattered most. This money. It had fangs.

But no matter all the things I did not know in 1976, I do know my mother never asked for my small-bill roll. She let me keep it safe, tight, locked. She let me build my autonomy, my dreams, my safety net, while she went out in the cold to wrap newspapers with co-workers only a few years older than I was.

Minimum wage in 1976 was $2.30 per hour. I didn't know about taxes and FICA and I didn't know that she would have to work almost sixty hours to take home as much as I had banded away. I didn't know the paper route was only four or five hours a week. I didn't know it would take almost three months to make that $110.00. Three months was 1/32 of my eight-year life.

I do know this: My mother never asked, and I never offered.

Raven

I see I see I see from sea to sea my mother cloaked in fear for me for my everlasting soul my role as son and father role as man diminished by my sickness and my weakness. My mother hated me for leaving hated my wife for taking and in that hating masked with love—or is it love that's masked with hate even now I am not sure—the only control she had left was to withhold.

Me

I withhold.

Raven

Yes.

Me

Not money. Not like her.

Raven

Not money not like her. Heart heart heart like her afraid and so protecting a defense a fence around her soul. To withhold is to not let go they sound different but they are the same. Think of those two things together when you try to find your way you think you know exactly what you don't let go of—

Me

You.

Raven

Me.

But, daughter, look, you think you know exactly what you don't let go of and that story keeps you stuck so turn it on its head and ask yourself what you're withholding now's the time you are unfolding into second life the patterns that you set up now might be the last ones you can make.

Me

I am greedy. I hold everything.

Raven

Tell me what they are and then explode them into dust.

Me

I hold time. Moments. Sleep. I withhold anger and love. I withhold myself.

Raven

What if I told you a bedtime story about your self would you think it bold would you think it greedy of me to tell you what I see that you cannot? You think your life is like a book you always loved your books your stories all the crimes and glories of the world contained within a cover held together with a spine but, daughter, glorious though books may be and certainly they help you help us find some light a book is only text and paper glue and spine nothing hooked until a reader picks it up and slips between the lines. This way a book is not one thing but many. This way a self is not one thing but many. When you lift its covers you find the spine has tentacles of possibilities reaching sea to sea to see the mistake that humans make is believing they are contained by front and back by single space and single spine with nothing else to give and be but what has already been inscribed.

Me

How do I know what stories are mine?

Raven

Daughter, moving from first life to second requires a good-night to small self a good-bye to all the layers you have painted on the pages of your flesh your sketches etched and scarred along your veins your pains the blood in which you swim not realizing you are swimming in a thing at all not realizing you are amphibious and can breathe below and breathe above it is so hard for you to know this truth with so much investment in the status quo but, daughter, first life yields to second life when you have mastered flowing to the deep and to the stars without a net to drag along the drops from where you've been.

Me

I hold moments. Spun around in the back seat waving good-bye to my first best friend, Donna, when we drove away from North Carolina. Standing in the corner of your hospital room on the morning you died. Crying on my apartment steps when he attacked me in the dark.

Raven

You know those moments coddled and cuddled those moments wrapped them in sacred swaddling clothes until they behaved exactly like you needed them to. You adorn your crown with those moments weave a veil out of those moments hold them up defiantly now that they're compliant they can illustrate your tale.

Tell me about him.

Me

_____.

Raven

Tell me about the one you turned to when I left the one you clung to when he told you you were not enough not smart enough not talented enough not enough not enough not enough caw—caw—caw and no one else would ever want you. The one you turned away from at first meeting turned back to when your grief was heating into lust and all that you could see to do was run. I saw I saw I saw so close was I so near but you had wrapped yourself in stones you scratched my name upon your bones and day by day you walled yourself away.

Tell me about him.

A memory is a commitment.

Me

I met him a few months before you died. He was with a friend of mine from high school. I had been holding on to high school, even though it had been a year since graduation.

I saw him and then forgot what I had seen.

Raven

What do you mean?

Me

I was repulsed by his demeanor, his cocksure walk and salesman smile. But after you died I was translucent and his strut and sneer looked like seduction not like lies. I saw and then I did not see.

Raven

From sea to sea I saw.

Me

I sent my intuition away.

Raven

Tell me, daughter, get out of your head and into your body your body that you have to both hold and release in order to live.

Me

After you died, he saw me broken. That's what abusers do. They find you when you're unsteady.

Raven

Tell me.

Me

If I'm going to tell you all the things he did to me, I have to tell you all the things I let him do. He didn't kidnap me or tie me down. Not even at the end. I went willingly, desperately, into him. That's a thing I've never said.

Raven

Tell me.

Me

I sought him out after you died. My whole body wanted to press against him and be consumed by him. I'd just broken up with my first love, the first person I'd slept with, and I had honestly thought we'd get married in that way you do when you're eighteen. After the break up, I'd spend precious seconds each morning before getting out of bed not remembering we weren't together anymore. Turns out that was good practice for your death a few months later. Those seconds of not-knowing or conscious-forgetting that bridged my dreams and day were the only moments in which I exhaled.

Your death made me horny. There's no polite way to say it. I wanted anyone and anything who would want me. For fifteen minutes. For a weekend. A month. A year. I didn't care. Young men have a particular kind of aliveness that feels invincible and immortal. Their angles and attitudes were off-putting before you died, but after—well, there was something to be said about someone who had unshakeable confidence in moving from point A to point B in the most direct manner. There was something to say about someone who was so bursting with life it was inconceivable that they would die. I wanted that to rub off on me. My body, which had been shedding her eggs since I was nine, was used to dying. Each month a potential life washed away, and even though I never wanted children, I felt the monthly dying nonetheless. The string of men I caught in the weeks after your death were as kind and meaningless to me as butterflies landing on petals. I wanted their lives and I drank them in like water.

I have always been greedy.

Raven

Tell me.

Me

None of them were interested in me, and that was fine because I could flit between them—my own insect wings unfolding just long enough to take what I needed and move on to the next scent. I was always going to control the leaving. I thought that was power. I thought moving from man-boy to boy-man made me a strong woman, an autonomous woman, and though I chose to do these things, I didn't choose them from a place of strength. I chose them from a place of fear.

Fear increased my avarice. I was greedy for life. For the world to see me as someone who was fine—who had everything pulled together—a job, an education, a fiancé. I was greedy for new skin, new hair, new voices in my head and in my bed. I cut and colored, permed and shaved my hair in the two years I was with him. I bought new clothes to fit the new, smaller, nearly invisible me. So many clothes my credit card bills soon revealed the depths of my greed—my fear—the size of the hole you left in my life that I was dying to fill.

I was afraid I would become invisible without you. You were the only one I thought could see me—the me underneath my high school Doc Martens and dark blue trench coat. The me beneath the black eyeliner and Malbec-lips. Because I believed you were the only one who could see me, I thought I needed the gaze of others to breathe at all. A shallow breath was better than none.

As my breath got smaller, I got smaller. 140 pounds to 120 pounds to 108 pounds, and as there was less of me, more men saw me, more men talked to me, more men wanted to protect me. My doctor congratulated me on losing so much weight. I finally fit in the height-weight chart that had confounded me since elementary school. Another doctor, thirty years later, would also congratulate me on my weight loss. "You look great! What are you doing?" he asked. "Cancer," I said, looking at him dead on.

I met the man I ran away to when I was at my smallest. A size 2, my clavicle a deep dip, my shoulder blades spikes. He was not a big man, but he was bigger than me, and when he wrapped his arms too tight around my chest, I felt relief that someone else was holding me up. I didn't have to try to stand. I had been holding the weight of your impending death for eleven years, and when you finally died the anticipation of it fled, and I fell backwards once that pack of stones was lifted. If it wasn't his arms that caught me, someone else's would have.

Raven

I see I see I see from sea to sea that you were lonely and for all these many years you have loathed yourself for that.

Me

When I graduated from high school, I was an unmoored boat. I didn't want you and Mom to come to the ceremony because I wanted to be free of everything, even you. Especially you. But the real reason is I couldn't risk anyone seeing you walking across the field because I couldn't remember what lie I had told to which friend.

At least one friend thought you were having a heart transplant. Another friend thought you were in hospice. I told someone else that my brother (you know I don't have a brother) who had served in Vietnam had never come home and just that week we got his dog tags back. I guess technically I could have had a brother who served in Vietnam (I was born in 1968 and you and Mom would have had to have met and hooked up when you both were nine, but you know, technicalities). Fortunately, I surrounded myself with people who were as poor at math as I was. Once I even brought a letter to my tenth-grade biology class that my fake-MIA brother had written to my mother. I wrote the letter with my left hand to disguise my handwriting and then heated it in the oven to turn the paper yellow.

I don't know why I didn't tell anyone the truth. There was a truth. You were dying. You had been dying since your heart attack in 1976. It was just getting closer and no one was talking about it, so that truth oozed like a pus in my throat, spreading lies coated in fear. The thing we didn't talk about crept out anyway in its own language.

Now that I've been a teacher for close to thirty years, I wonder why none of my own teachers noticed anything. Maybe they did and didn't know what to do. It had to have been obvious I was using stage makeup. But I'm sure there have been students I have failed to reach, failed to give a space to speak. I look out at my classes sometimes, so young, most the age I was when you died, and my heart cracks for them and even for me a little.

Raven

I saw you leaving me before I left you and it made all the sense in all the world and I wanted to reach for you and hold you back I wanted to keep you trapped inside the house because every day that passed meant one less day that we would spend together.

Me

I knew that and I wanted to stay and go at the same time. I felt your stickiness and I couldn't climb out of it fast enough. I've spent the last three decades trying to find it again. The last three decades holding on to what I couldn't wait to get away from.

Raven

I spent most days moving from bed to couch to bed to couch in conversation with the cat and the God I'd tried so hard to find but neither one talked back.

Me

I loved being a part of the theatre club because there was always something to do. Every afternoon after school. Most weekends. Some evenings. I could be away from home from six to six. I didn't have to see you failing.

I'm sorry.

Raven

Yes.

Me

I was relieved when you died.

Raven

I was relieved when I died.

14

The scientific method allows us to run ideas through a series of tests—of checks and balances—before we end up publishing our findings and having to stand behind them and build a career from them. The scientific method is supposed to, through its repetition and stringent peer review process, prevent us from forming conclusions based only off our own biases. It hopefully prevents us from causing harm to others, living myopically, and letting one rogue idea take over an entire field of study. It provides assurances that theories, once they reach the point of public dissemination, have been challenged and modified until a majority of qualified individuals come to the same, reproducible conclusion.

It's not perfect.

But it's a start.

"Everything is fine," says my mother, except she wasn't at home when I got up that Saturday morning to prove it. I woke up to our neighbor, Mrs. Hicks, smoking a cigarette and staring into the kitchen. My mother comes home that afternoon and tells me we're going to the beach to stay with my aunt. "No, Daddy can't come right now. No, he's resting. Don't worry. Everything is fine."

I will be eight in six days. I am excited to be a round number—a number that looks like a woman, all grown up with hips and belly. For my birthday, we were going to go to Carowinds, the low-rent version of Six Flags, on the outskirts of Charlotte. Not the beach. But I'm confused. We don't do things spontaneously. We plan and we are prepared so there are no surprises, but now we are taking a surprise trip to the Atlantic and we are going without Daddy and Mrs. Hicks hugs my mother too long on her way out the back door.

My mother stops in the tiny kitchen, rests her arm against the harvest gold refrigerator. Her eyes are red but she smiles. "Did you eat?" she says. "I can make eggs."

"Where is Daddy?"

"He needed to go somewhere so he could rest."

"Where?"

"Somewhere quiet."

"Why?"

She cracks two eggs into my favorite Minnie Mouse bowl even though I didn't tell her I wanted them and I wasn't hungry. Even though it's afternoon and eggs are for morning. She spins them with a fork, drops in some milk, pours them into the cold frying pan. "Oh my," she says. "I forgot to turn the stove on." Her laugh sounds like gravel. "Why don't you go get dressed and I'll help you pack for the beach. Won't that be fun? You can have your birthday at the ocean."

"I wanted to go to Carowinds. Where's Daddy?"

She turns the stove on and the eggs and butter snap. "We need to leave really soon, honey, so I can get back before dark."

"I'll stay with you." I am almost eight, almost a full-figured woman, and my mother has forgotten how to make eggs.

⋘

Here's a bare-bones scientific method that anyone past fifth grade should have learned.

1) Observe some aspect of the universe.

2) Invent a tentative description, called a hypothesis, that is consistent with what you have observed.

3) Use the hypothesis to make predictions.

4) Test those predictions by experiments or further observations and modify the hypothesis in the light of your results.

5) Repeat steps 3 and 4 until there are no discrepancies between the theory and experiment and/or observation.

This is very useful to scientists because it ensures that no one rogue idea gains traction in the field. It assures us that multiple reproducible experiments finding the same conclusions have been done before we dare to accept a theory as fact.

It also provides the illusion of infallibility. It allows for the confirmation bias to creep in—in other words, the tendency for us to interpret new evidence and information through the lens of our already solidified beliefs. Again, the scientific method is not perfect.

But it's a start.

When we look at a life through the lens of the scientific method, we emphasize its weakest links. We use the confirmation bias. Hindsight bias. Our implicit and explicit biases. We rarely engage in effective peer review. In life, our scientific method-reached theories aren't challenged by a prestigious journal. They aren't competing for grant funding or tenure. They are never double-blind studies. When we latch onto a misguided theory about the way the world works, we tend to hold on to it all the way through to its destructive conclusion. And because of our human desire to be right and our superhuman ability to ignore information that conflicts with our conclusions, we can hold onto false theories even when rivers of contradictory evidence are overflowing into our lives.

I observe that my mother's spine is rigid. Her knuckles tense white around the spatula and her voice levels. "You can't stay with me. Your aunt is expecting you. Won't that be fun?"

I didn't think it would. My aunt uses three forks at every meal and her tablecloths are white linen and should never have crumbs on them. When she took us to the beach before, she spent the whole time under a big white umbrella wrapped in pale blue cotton. She always said she'd watch me in the ocean, but she wore fly's-eyes sunglasses and had a thick book in front of her nose and I didn't believe she wanted to watch me at all.

"Don't forget your bathing suit," says my mother, and I see the tiniest of shakes start to shimmy up her spine and it scares me because she is always solid, so I run to my room and pull out my red-and-white-checkered one-piece, still damp from our trip to the pool yesterday. I should put it in a plastic bag but don't.

⛀

Humans are information absorbing machines. We are constantly taking in the sights, sounds, textures, and smells of our world and making meaning out of them. We're analyzing them, filtering them, judging and deciding what is useful and what isn't. What is good for us and what is dangerous. Our foundational operating system takes root in childhood. What we concretize in our early years informs every other developmental stage. Even without the tool of language, infants are sorting, cataloging, aligning, rejecting and accepting input from the world around them and, yes, again without language, making stories out of them—making *meaning* out of them. And those meanings, those stories about how they have determined that Their World operates, burrow into the subconscious and whisper ways to navigate the world as they grow.

⛀

I hear Mom scraping eggs onto a plate, so I creep across the hall into my parents' bedroom to look for Daddy. Everything seems fine—his pants from yesterday are hung across the closet door, his wallet weighting the back pocket like a stone. His keys, a jumble of silver and gold, are on the dresser next to a red golf tee. Their bathroom still smells of Mennen and his yellow toothbrush still leans in the glass on the sink. His shoes, the right one boosted two inches to accommodate his polio-eaten leg, are beside the bed. Where could he be if he left all these parts of him here?

"Honey? Come, let's eat."

I grab his Timex, a silver one with a thick band that closed around his wrist like a jaw. It still ticks. The date is still today. Everything must be fine if the hands are moving forward. He called it a timepiece, not a watch, and he wound it every night so it would stay precise. I check again. The second-hand clicks. The hour is accurate. He would have wound it just last night. There was still time left on it. I put the watch on my wrist but it slides off onto the shag carpet. I go to my room to place it on my bed next to Carl the Red Dragon. I assume that something bad had happened to Dad because he left his watch behind. I've never seen him out of the house without it.

Mom has forgotten the juice that goes in the Hamburgler glass, but I don't say anything. I eat my eggs even though it's afternoon and eggs are for morning. She didn't make any for herself. She's wiping her hands over and over on the dishtowel when the kitchen phone rings and she freezes. Two rings. Three. I reach for it.

"No!" she says too fast and too loud, and I squeeze my eyes so I don't cry because she never says anything too loud.

⌘

When we reach adulthood, we often run into trouble when an early belief system comes into conflict with a goal we are pursuing. Until that point of conflict, we rarely consider what stories might be lurking in the understory of our operating system. We're often not sure where those early beliefs came from, and we definitely don't remember choosing, "Yes, I'll have this belief system today," or "No, thank you, not this one." We absorb and absorb and absorb everything from our contexts, and because we are animals, our biology kicks in here too with our imperative physical needs. This means the larger people who are feeding and housing us when we're infants and children have a disproportionate amount of influence over the stories we take in. They, too, may not be saying, "Look, this is how things are," (though sometimes they do), but they will be interacting with each other and with us in ways that will influence what we internalize about our new world. They will be contributing authors to our stories.

⌘

Mom holds the receiver in her hand. "Hello?" Then, "Go in the other room, honey." I don't go because I am almost eight and I can hear whatever it is she is not telling me. But I don't learn anything. All she says are yesses and nos and a quick, "I'll be right there."

I can't tell if she's mad at me for sitting there, watching her

109

twist the beige cord between her fingers. "Go next door and see if Mrs. Hicks can come back," she says, and I slide off the chair. Her voice is too quiet and soft for no reason.

She's already waiting in the Buick with her pocketbook when I return with Mrs. Hicks. We wave good-bye to her and I go to my room where I hold the Timex, the minute-hand a tick-click-pause, and I wind it tight so that time will not run out. I determine that if his watch will stay alive, he will also stay alive.

✍

Human growth is about uncovering those unconscious belief systems and consciously determining whether or not they're of value to us anymore. When we find ourselves in crisis moments in later life, we're often in conflict with one of those early stories we told ourselves about how the world works. Through our struggles, we're finding that a belief system we hold isn't serving us anymore, or isn't allowing us to actually achieve the things we claim we want, so we have to 1) figure out what that belief system is, and 2) do the necessary work of unpacking it and revising it to something that is useful.

✍

After I have been shuffled away to Wilmington, North Carolina, to the two-story home of my linen-wearing aunt, I learn that Dad had a heart attack and was in intensive care. No one tells me what a heart attack is, so I imagine bullies, like Thackston in my second-grade class, beating up on his heart until it is crying, blood leaking onto the floor. I remember there had been a patch of blood on the carpet in Mom and Dad's bedroom. I worry about who might sneak under my ribcage and attack my heart, and I wonder if they will use baseball bats like I'd seen boys doing on the playground.

I'm not allowed to visit Dad because children are not allowed in the ICU ward, so I also make up a story about where he is and what has happened. I'm left with no choice. With only minimal information, I have to fill in the gaps based on my limited eight-year-old experience. I can write him letters, Mom says, so I do because writing makes things make sense.

110

Dear Daddy,

I miss you. I have your watch. I will keep it wound so that time won't run out.

Love,

Laraine

≈

Scientific method implementation through a young child's lens:

1) Observe some aspect of the universe.

Dad isn't here. Something is wrong. His clothes are here. Mom is acting weird.

Notice how hard it is to isolate a single aspect of the universe, as would be the intention in a research lab. In our lives, every aspect we observe is informed by its context.

2) Invent a hypothesis.

Dad has died. It's the only thing that makes sense. Why wouldn't anyone tell me if he just went to the golf course or went somewhere for work? Mom says everything is fine but I'm seeing something different. I'm feeling something different. Mom says it's all okay. She is big and I am small, so she knows more than I do.

Conclusion: I cannot trust my intuition.

This incorrect conclusion isn't Mom's fault. I could attempt to write this scene from her point of view, knowing that her husband had a massive heart attack in the middle of the night, knowing that he was in ICU and that the chances of him pulling through the week were slim, knowing that she might be left alone at thirty-six with a young child, knowing she had to do whatever was necessary to protect us and to keep the family afloat. I could write her side in a way that would make you completely understand why "everything is fine" was a logical thing to say. The message I internalized from her trying to protect me is not her fault.

But it's still there.

≈

In writing a memoir or a novel, it's important to know what your protagonist's key misbeliefs are—to use a term coined by

111

Lisa Cron in her book *Story Genius*. Those misbeliefs, because they are part of a character's operating system, help fuel their actions. Those actions tend to get them into trouble, because in good storytelling (perhaps not so much in life) drama is essential to creating a compelling narrative. If no one is coming into conflict with anything, then there's not going to be a lot of tension or reason for the reader to invest in the work. In good storytelling, the external conflicts are triggering the internal conflicts, and it's those internal conflicts that our protagonist must resolve in order to grow and move forward. In life, those misbeliefs are our faulty conclusions—the meanings we make about how the world works.

In building a life, most of us get about halfway through step four of the scientific method before a breakdown occurs. Rigorously challenging our theories is a hard sell. Let me illustrate.

As a writer, it's clear to me that I cannot see my own work unbiased, and I need to employ the assistance of others to help make it as coherent as possible. I know that, though I may be attached to a particular story idea or concept, it might not play out the way I've envisioned, and I have to be willing to let go of my original premise so that what is trying to be born can breathe. I didn't know this when I first started writing. Like most young writers, I thought I knew what I was doing. I have come to realize I have no idea, but the writing knows a bit more than I do, and with help, I can say something. But there's a substantial difference between me as a writer and me as just, well, me.

Me as me has a much more difficult time recognizing my own biases. I'm challenged when I remember that the world is millions of worlds, not just my own, and that my lens is not even a single clear lens, but rather a fractured one—one that has looked at something too closely and been shattered, one that has been dented and crunched and colored. Even if I know my lens is flawed, I can't see the flaws, or I see them and I quickly overwrite them with a herculean logic-dance to make sure that I uphold my own righteous right-ness. I don't know if it's possible for a human being to have a completely clean lens—a view that is detached and present and laser-focused in its landscapes.

This detachment is what I suspect enlightened means, but I don't know if there can be a human with no filter. I used to think "waking up" in the existential sense was about divesting myself from all of these layers of story, but I no longer feel that way. I feel those layers are precisely what makes us human—it's the price and privilege of this incarnation. A human being is a story, and if we lose the fundamentals of story that make us up, who are we? Who can we be if we are not in relationship to our experiences and—here's the big point—the meaning we've made of those experiences?

As a writer, I rely on these filters, and these filters shape my characters, their journeys, and their transformations. My stories in this book need a filter so the reader can be rooted in a context. When writing fiction, I ask these questions of my characters: How do you see the world? How are you shaped by it? How were you wounded by it? How were you scarred and how did you take those scars into the world with you and impact others with them? Understanding the answers to those questions helps me build dimensional characters that readers can relate to. A character with none of these things—no personal mythology, no wounding of self or others, no doubling down on false rightness—wouldn't hold anyone's interest on the page. In a memoir, even a speculative one like this, I must ask these questions of myself.

When I get home from visiting my aunt at the beach, Daddy is home again, but the whole house has been turned upside down. Everything is in the same place, but nothing is right. Daddy is in bed in a dark bedroom. He isn't going to work. He isn't grilling steaks on the Hibachi. Mom is still making eggs, still pouring bowls of Cheerios, still brewing coffee on the stove. She is still smiling her wide beautiful smile, but it isn't in her eyes anymore, just her lips. She folds the laundry, cleans the bathrooms, vacuums the carpets. Daddy's chest is black and blue and there's a jagged vertical scar dividing it. He doesn't eat chocolate ice cream. He doesn't smoke his Pall Malls. I line my stuffed animals up in my bedroom across the hall from Mom and Dad's and I start to practice what I will say when he is gone. My kitty-cat trashcan fills with Kleenex and nobody asks me if I'm all right, which is okay because I would have said everything is fine, I just had a cold; everything is fine, I just have allergies; everything is fine.

❧

Forty years later, I notice the blood in the toilet. By this time, I have crafted a gold-medal-worthy ability to ignore what is right in front of me. It's early October. It's just a little bit of blood. It could be anything. It could be a slight rectal tear. I Googled it (something I will quickly learn to never ever do). An anal fissure. A hemorrhoid, most likely. Nothing to worry about. I actively did not see the WebMD warning to see a doctor immediately if it does not go away. I actively did not see the last entry on possible causes: cancer.

Instead, I go to the bathroom in the dark and flush the toilet without looking and over a month passes and it becomes December and my husband and I are in Las Vegas and I'm in the bathroom at the Cosmopolitan Casino after being unable to eat lunch and the blood is leaking out of me like I'm a faucet. I sit there in the fancy bathroom listening to the fancy women in their high Manolo Blahniks and Hermes scarves talking about the things fancy women talk about.

I have never been a fancy woman. We come to Vegas because it's an easy drive from Prescott, Arizona, where we live. It's such an other-worldly world that we quickly forget about things for a while. We like the food and the theatre and the spectacle. We don't gamble. We don't drink. I take up too much space for the shops that cater to the fancy women who are size zeroes and can walk miles in their fancy shoes, so we don't shop much. The irony isn't lost on me that I don't gamble in Vegas,

114

but I've been gambling ever since fall—that rectal bleeding was not only okay, but was no big deal and would go away. Even with my poor math skills, my luck would have been better at the blackjack tables.

I don't have a pad with me so I roll up bunches of the fancy-lady toilet paper and try to catch the bleeding. I can't stay in here forever. My husband is waiting in the lobby. "Something is wrong," I tell him, and he just nods. He knew about the bleeding, but we both played this insane game of chicken over the past month. "Only a little blood tonight!" I'd say.

"Oh, good," he'd say. "It's getting better!"

On Christmas Eve we are snowed in watching bad horror films on Netflix when the blood flows onto the sheets. I didn't even have to go to the bathroom. The blood just leaked. I am flying out the next week to teach a workshop in Massachusetts. On the way to the airport I ask Mom, "Have you ever had rectal bleeding?"

"A little," she says. "Why? Are you having it?"

"A little." I wear only black pants now. I have extra thick, extra long pads.

"It's probably nothing."

"Probably."

When I get back home, I call to make an appointment with my primary care provider to begin the health care journey to get to a specialist. When the specialist, a gastroenterologist, meets with me after my colonoscopy in February, which revealed colon cancer, his first question is, "What took you so long to see me?"

I want to say it's because it took four weeks to get into his office. (True.) But that's not the whole truth. The whole truth is because I looked at bright red toilet water for four months and convinced myself it was okay. It was fine.

Because I didn't know what to do if it wasn't.

115

Me

My mother, ever always fine, became a shadow of substance. When she returned to your hospital room after receiving the call that you had died, she touched your curled hand and left. I watched. I didn't hear her say anything. I didn't see her cry, though I felt my throat turning inside out with unsaid words. She signed paperwork. She drove us to Burger King. She and I picked out a coffin. I wrote your epitaph: *He walked by faith*, referring to your polio, your first trauma, your first betrayal.

I never saw her collapse. Never saw her stop. Never saw her miss more than a few days of work the week of your death. I never saw her blink or pause or ask for help from anyone, and so I watched and swallowed and never asked for help and never stopped and never touched her and never asked how she was doing and never thought someone should ask me how I was doing. I was fine. She was fine. We were fine.

Raven

I see I see I see from sea to sea and, daughter, you did not see. Your mother, my friend, my wife, she carried all my rage and all my grief for all our time together all our time. She took me into her solid bones her wide hips her stunning smile she took me in and held me where no one else had. She saw my anger strut-strut-strutting putt-putt-putting across the golf course where I raged and won and walked yes I walked hear that polio hear ye hear ye I walked and my anger did not push her away. She was strong enough to stay to hear me gasping for breath in the night to hear me crying to touch my attacked heart with her fingertips and cool it down enough to keep beating keep pumping keep loving.

She had practice, your mother my friend my wife. Her own mother, an alcoholic, her own childhood spent absorbing the

116

grief of her mama the rage of her mama the betrayal of her mama. Her skeleton danced when others would have broken.

You did not see her hold my shirts to her nose in the dark corner of the closet when you were running running gone. You did not see her wash them all and fold them into perfect stacks to donate. You saw her giving me away. You saw her forgetting about me, but she had me in her bones, you see, daughter, you see you see. Beneath her skin I stayed.

She walked the aisles of the fluorescent grocery store on Friday nights because to be home alone was loud so she picked up and put back oranges, bananas, and melons. She carted my favorite meat and then remembered I would not eat but she bought it anyway and when it turned she tossed it out until the next Friday when she could bring it home again. She kept the saccharine I'd used to sweeten my tea in the cupboard for years one day one day she might drink tea again one day she might drop the white capsules in a pitcher of Lipton and pour a glass and sit on the patio and ask me how I'm doing one day one day.

The evenings were worse than the mornings. The mornings had purpose had work had action had living had proof that she was still as solid as she was before but evenings cracked and stretched and whispered. She lay in our bed her head on her pillow her body on her side of the bed but I would dream her hold her touch her and she would wake up on my side her life side on my death side her warm arms clutching the sheets that no longer smelled of me.

That year she lost an inch of height my weight in her bones my rage in her bones my love in her bones that year she lost an inch of height, my daughter, the year you lost sixty pounds the year my family tried to meet me meet me but none of you could see each other none of you could reach each other only me only me only me could hold you all beneath my slick black wings only me could see.

I left. I had nowhere to go so I left to go nowhere. Nowhere had a name and a face, but it has taken me decades to speak it, to see it, to share it. I don't quite know how to explain it to you. Maybe I should back up.

When we left North Carolina to move to Arizona, I had no language for the loss. To this day, I can't make rational sense of the palpable pain I felt when we drove away down Springfield Drive. I was facing behind us, looking back, always looking back, waving at my friend Donna who was watching from the street. We waved until we couldn't see each other anymore and then I wailed. I'm sorry that I was so loud, I am, but I'm not sorry that I let you know how much I hurt. I didn't see what I see now, that you were moving toward something, or so you'd hoped, not away. But I refused to take my soul with me when we moved and you recognized that. You tried to connect with me, but I was lost.

I locked myself in my bedroom with the dark sunshades to keep out the Phoenix sun, and I listened to Casey Kasem's *American Top 40* and I cried to all the songs. It didn't help that I was thirteen and exploding with hormones. It didn't help that even though no one mentioned it, we all knew we had come West for you to die. It didn't help that we all closed ourselves in our rooms and ached.

We pulled into Phoenix in late July, 1981, into an unimaginable 115-degree day. Phoenix was flat and carpeted in concrete and the trees were thin and thirsty. *I will not die in this place*, I vowed then, and twenty-two years later when I moved north to Prescott, I remembered that pledge.

But that move to Prescott was a different leaving. A choice. A decision born from hope. That's not the leaving I'm avoiding telling you about.

When you died, I left my mother alone in the cement and the heat. All my anchors were gone. I had already moved out of the house because I was desperate to be an adult. I had chosen to attend a community college instead of going to a university so I would be nearby when you died and I wanted at least the illusion of being grown up. You were mad that I turned down scholarships to college. You thought I was throwing my life away and I saw the disappointment in your face. I saw how I was not becoming the daughter you had raised, how I was not fulfilling the dreams you had for me, but I was, don't you see, I was.

A daughter is a commitment.

I could not go away to school. I could have if you'd have had the courtesy to die when I was eight when you had your first heart attack. Or if you'd have managed to wait until I was thirty or forty or fifty, but that wasn't how it was to be. You died when I was nineteen with one foot in childhood and one foot in adulthood, and though I had wanted little else since moving to Arizona than to leave it, I could not leave you.

You knew that. But still you were disappointed. Still you were angry that my life was in a holding pattern for you.

Neither one of us could speak the truth. The risk was too great. If I told you that I was staying close by to be there for you, you would have broken. It is one thing to think you know why a person does something. It is another thing entirely to be certain. If you knew I had stayed for you, you would have felt less than. You would have felt weak and ashamed and you would have added my choices to your list of regrets. You already felt minimized because of your polio-eaten leg. Your half-heart. Your inability to work and earn money and go places with us. You were already too brutalized by your life. I could not emasculate you more.

If you told me that you knew I was staying for you, you would have had to acknowledge that you were dying. It is one thing to think you know a person is dying. It is another thing entirely to be certain.

So we held the tension between us.

A family is a commitment.

Raven

Stop stop stop stop stop. I cannot hear it now I cannot hear it still I will not hear it now but I know, daughter, I know. Your

119

mother and I we prayed and prayed she prayed I prayed we sought answers where we'd always looked before and came up empty. Should we move or should we stay? Her home was not Southern. She had spent her days trying to be Southern trying to fit in with my family and their expectations of suppers and gardens and quilting and visiting but she was not Southern she was her own.

I underestimated how your cells had attached to the red Piedmont mud how your hair still clung to the oak branches how your fingers entangled in moss I know, daughter, I know.

A place is a commitment.

I have left my own fingers laced tight in Southern spiders' webs, my own cells mixed in sandy soil.

I did not want to go go go fly away across the country but I could not stay they were coming for me my family they were coming for me and I couldn't let them have me I had already sacrificed so much. We didn't talk squawk chatter-chat-chatter we lobbed verses at each other we used God and Jesus and the sweet by and by as weapons and I was so very tired of being told I was not enough not saved not repentant not worthy because I had been weak enough to bring my sicknesses upon me I cannot tell you how much the weight of their religion crushed my bones how much their sanctimony scalded my scabs and bled me dry. I knew I knew I knew you were breaking when we were driving away I saw you waving I saw you dropping tears along the road and, daughter, I see I see I see from sea to sea and you are there still on Springfield Drive, salt water up to your neck standing on your tiptoes waving goodbye goodbye goodbye.

Me

I have frozen myself at several points in my life, and when I scan my past those moments are locked inside snow globes, suspended memory malignancies that glow pink on a screen. I go for scans now every six months. My upper abdominal area. My pelvic region. A colonoscopy every year. Wait. I'm skipping too far ahead. We aren't to that chapter yet. I don't want to talk about it, not how cancer manifested, not how it shocked me, not how it made me look back at these frozen snowy malignancies and blow fire on them stoked with cold rage until they melted and ran liquid in my blood. I don't want to talk about any of the things I've never talked about.

Cancer is a commitment.

Raven

From where I perch there is no yesterday today tomorrow only you and me and all that see only you and me. I'll go first because it hurts it hurts it hurts to perch and be unable to reach you I beseech you look at what is locked away it stays so quiet but it beats it beats it beats against the sides of your colon waiting for you to hear it so it does not have to spear the wall and swim to other organs bide your time, my daughter, at your own risk tsk tsk your own risk.

You've encased those moments in a shell encapsulated their dividing cells but you have not transformed them into action you have not released the traction that has held them simmering waiting waiting waiting for you to notice they are there baiting you with cramps and blood until you look and lift the glass and hear their frozen stories waking up your hidden rage your hidden power take this chance, my daughter, lift the glass.

Me

I cannot look. Not at all the globes, all the moments, just the ones I've memorized and now carry on my skin. I can look at when we left North Carolina and when you had your heart attack and when you died and even a little glance at when I got cancer but I cannot look at what lies between. I cannot look, but I can say this:

Where were you?

Raven

Caw! Caw! Caw! I screech to reach you then but then is now is always now because your body is a record and the grooves that you have made skip and skip and skip their notes until the vinyl cracks and the music spills into all the cells and all you can say then is you should have lifted the needle should have raised the glass should have mended the melody before the notes clash and fade to black.

I did not leave you, daughter, did not leave you held me here I held me here and I am feather and fire now feather on wire and I did not leave you did not leave. But there is more than you can see I see I see more than you can see your snow globe moments your malignant cells your body breaking from the weight of all you have tried to hold no more waiting, daughter, no more waiting time is up and we must see must see beyond the glass, daughter—it is breaking anyway—it is best that you control the crash.

Me

Where were you?

Raven

I said take care of your mother stay strong be strong because I knew that I was dying and I knew you would be the one to hold it all together but I didn't know, daughter, that the holding would turn on you turn on all of us because you didn't know how to ask for help didn't know how to be dependent on any-one and your mother and I didn't teach you each of us our own independent volcanoes erupting only alone. How could you have seen what to do how could you have seen how to break but not be broken how could you have known a way besides the closing down of feeling besides the stuffing deep inside your body how could you have known a better way and now I perch here chit-chat-chattering and I am begging you to lift the glass pour your fury on the snow and watch it melt, daughter daughter, you can die of both fire and of ice.

You always cried when Frosty died his corncob pipe and his button nose floating in a puddle of water, daughter, Frosty sang and danced and embraced his impermanent icy form but still you cried when the sun came out and the credits rolled.

Me

I was thinking of you. I was imagining you melting.

Raven

I know.

Me

_____.

Raven

_____.

Me

I wanted him to stay.

Raven

_____.

Me

He didn't live very long at all.

Raven

None of us do.

Me

I could have died.

Raven

Yes.

Me

Twice. Once in the snow globe and once with cancer. I watched the blood pour from the darkest parts of me and I flushed it away and went to work. I saw I saw I saw but did not see.

Raven

I saw I saw I saw I came to you. See, daughter, see.

Me

If I lift the snow globe's glass, then what is inside will have happened and I am not the kind of woman to whom these things happen. I am not that person. I am strong enough to survive it and strong enough to keep quiet about it.

Raven

But, daughter, it has woken up and it is coming for you. Meet it first I beg you meet it first.

Me

I would rather talk about surgery, talk about cancer, talk about waking up in the recovery room, talk about anything at all than what is under that glass, that globe, that encapsulated tumor.

Raven

It is waking up it is waking up it is waking up meet it meet it meet it let me take you there.

Me

It is gone. They took the tumor out. It's gone.

Raven

Yes but if you don't come back with me if you don't let me see you face it then there might be—

Me

No! Be quiet. It is gone.

Raven

The conditions in which that tumor grew must change so that it can't find a place find its space find a trace of who you used to be so it can disappear. A surgeon's knife only cuts away what it can see but I see, daughter, I see from sea to sea and you must tell me take me help me show me what happened what you shadowed cloaked encapsulated so we can build again. Please, daughter, let me save you now.

Me

I do not need saving.

Raven

Caw! Caw! My fault bad choice of words I cannot shake off all my old religion you need not saving child but resurrecting and I need resurrecting too these feathers this beak these wings they are not salvation not redemption no intention to stay this way a bird a ghost a haunted haunter I need resurrecting I was not supposed to stay but cancer woke you up and brought me back from the branches where I've watched for thirty years I watched but could not intervene could not do anything at all was useless dead as I was living weak and dying weak and hiding just how close to the end I was.

Please take me back with you.

Me

I looked for you everywhere.

Raven

I am here.

Me

No. You are still not here. You're in-between and that's not good enough. That's never been good enough. You keep pushing me and I don't want to see. But it's coming. I feel the water rushing in my bones. I can't let it go, I can't. It will drown me.

Raven

Daughter, you are drowning now if you ignore the water you will falter, daughter, you will not know you're falling will not know you cannot breathe until you're gone and if you go while I am in-between how will I find you again how will we fix this life how if you are drowning will you live?

You must recognize the water so you can float.

Me

_____.

15

Two years to the week after my resection surgery, I return to Tucson for the Tucson Festival of Books. But that's not why I'm going. It's never why I'm going. It's a reconnaissance mission. One more attempt to rescue myself from incessantly roaming the streets around the University of Arizona. It's not the college that pulls me. So much of it is unrecognizable thirty years later. But Tucson is held by the Catalina Mountains and the Santa Rita Mountains, and those look just like they did in 1987 when I arrived with D—, erasing and reinventing myself with every mile away from Phoenix. I would erase the Girl Whose Dad Died and become College Student with a Boyfriend. I would morph into someone no one could recognize and in months and miles I would be all right.

D— was repellant to me when I first saw him, cocky and slick, a poster boy for a player. But Dad hadn't died yet, so my vision was still clear. When I met him a second time, just a week after Dad's death, cocky became seductive, slick became charming. Regardless, he represented escape. A chance to be in my body again.

Did you know that when a person is grieving, they can leave their body? They move through days, drive cars, go to work, but they're not there. They've gone on with the person they loved, and it happened so quickly and so quietly they didn't realize it until they had been gone for so long there was no clear path back. The body had kept moving, but without a soul to navigate it, it got lost. It's so easy—so logical—to keep going with the dead. Everything makes sense there. Or, even if it doesn't, you're not grieving there. You're home.

My transformation to College Student with a Boyfriend progressed seamlessly. I'd come out of four years of high school theatre and two years of community college theatre. I knew how to step into a part. When I sat in the eight a.m. seminars in the lower level of the Modern Languages Building, in desks that had been there for forty years, I drank in the smell of old wood and paper. This is Life, I thought. This is the Point of It All. I haunted thrift stores searching for clothes to represent this role—long flowing skirts and peasant tops, Birkenstock sandals, plastic chunky jewelry. These were supposed to be the best years of my life and that could only happen if I had all the things—boyfriend, apartment, job, good GPA.

I always had all the things. I always exceeded expectations. Kids hung out at Gentle Ben's and Fiddlee Fig, had late night coffees at Bentley's, danced at the bar at the Hotel Congress, but I didn't do those things because the Boyfriend wasn't what I thought and I had stayed so long without a soul in my body that I didn't notice when I lost myself.

D— followed me. Registered for exactly the same classes I did. Waited for me to get off work, while somehow never being willing to work himself. I had to keep buying new clothes at the thrift stores because every week I lost more weight. Every week I grew smaller until I reached ninety-five pounds at five foot two and my gynecologist was gleeful that I finally fit in the weight box for my height. Disappearing was rewarded at every turn. Who needed a body anyway, when with each pound I lost I moved closer to Dad.

An energy healer I worked with after my cancer diagnosis suggested that D— caused my cancer. Causality is extremely difficult to prove in any situation, and though I don't agree with that causality, I can find some correlations—not so much that D— did anything methodically to conjure up malignant cells, but that during my time with him, and in the thirty years since, I have energetically held on to the shame of our time together and the disconnection from the person I had pretended to be. It wasn't him. But perhaps there was a relationship between the way I treated myself, and the way I let myself be treated, that turned toxic over time. I lived in Tucson a disintegrated person, and every time I return to the city, I try to piece myself back together.

Every trip I think *I'll just touch this classroom door where I first read Toni Morrison; I'll just walk up these stairs to the student union; I'll just eat at The Blue Willow on Campbell where I went every Saturday morning after D— and I broke up and eat a breakfast burrito at the table beside the kitchen and I'll be made whole.* But I'm never there to catch. I walk down Stone Avenue past the Rialto Theater where I pretended to be a normal college kid at an Ani diFranco concert, but I'm not there. I haunt the Fourth Avenue arts district, where I bought the brown and white thrift store sofa from the Salvation Army, found feminism in Antigone's Books, and shaved my head at The Coyote Wore Sideburns. I'm never there, though the places slot into familiar grooves in my memory and I feel comfort and displacement—I am home but I am not. It could be 1987 or 2019 in any of these places. My body makes no distinction. But the places that I think are holding me are empty, and the gap inside me aches.

In the immediate months after surgery, I woke up multiple times a night to eliminate solid waste. I could not sleep through the night. My body was compelled to expel what it didn't need. "The gut doesn't much like to be messed with," said a friend. "It operates below consciousness. It is slow to accept change." The whole process was so slow I woke fully up every few hours and when I'd try to return to sleep, I felt fearful. I imagined malignant colon cells hiding in the dark waiting for the moment I stopped being vigilant, waiting for the chance to surprise me once again with the ways the things we repress can attack us without warning. I didn't know the cancer was there, so how could I know when it returned? How could I know if it came back?

I have two deeply embedded operating stories for my life:

1) The dead do not stay dead.

2) Once I am given something, I hold onto it no matter what.

Both of these stories represent the toxic side of loyalty and commitment. Both of these stories are rooted in fear. Cancer may have been cut out, but it will return. My father died, but the ghost I have made of him lives on. I was diagnosed with cancer, so I can never let that go. I loved a father, so if I allow that relationship to change, I have let him down. I must remember him always, all minutes, all days. I must freeze him, like my tumor cells have been frozen in a lab in Scottsdale, Arizona.

I returned to therapy after my diagnosis. My ability to imagine and create stories had turned on me. My therapist uses a Jungian-based music therapy approach called the Bonny Method of Guided Imagery. This approach, for me, is profoundly helpful. It allows me to use story and metaphor—the language of symbols—to unpack my own hidden things. Each session we create a question or idea to explore into, and then I move into a semi-trance state and journey, using the movement of the music to help uncover the underlying patterns. "I can't sleep," I told my therapist. "I panic. My gut won't rest. It's lost." And so we began to tunnel into that and the image that arrived was a school of shimmering fish swimming clockwise in my belly. The fish know this pattern well. They are hardwired to swim in this way.

After surgery, twelve inches of my colon was removed. No one consulted with the fish. No one asked the cells around the tumor how they felt about the forced removal of a part of their system. The knives were cold and the cuts were precise and swift and before the fish could understand what was happening, their path had been repurposed, their familiar pool bloodied and screaming, but even the screams were muted with morphine. Even the pain—the signal that something important has happened—was transmogrified to "fine."

"What do the fish want?" asked my therapist.

"They don't understand—they don't know what happened. They want their fish friends back. When they took that part of me, they took some of the fish and so the fish keep swimming back, keep looking for what they lost. They don't know where to go."

Raven's Father

Son, I feel like a rat in a maze. I reach out—arms wider than they ever were in life—and my fingertips graze a concave surface on each side. I am contained in spherical translucence. If I jump, my head makes soft impact. If I lie down, I sink. Not enough to get stuck, but enough to leave an imprint. When I get up, my impression dissolves like footsteps in mud.

I'm nearing the Cape Fear Memorial Bridge heading west out of Wilmington, and through these blurred walls, I see familiar things. The water is beneath me, gray dotted with whitecaps. Beside me, the traffic moves, folks in their own colored plastic bubbles. Remember how you used to love to get stuck on the bridge when the big boats came through? The sides of the bridge fit together like a jaw, opening and closing, opening and closing. "Daddy," you said. "How does the bridge stay open?" I didn't have an answer, but I should have tried. So many times I stayed silent.

When I look back on my life—though it's puzzling—I am still *here*—so is this death or is death life turned inside out? No matter. When I look back on when I was outside this maze, I can see that there were always clues as to which road to take. Like this one: I should have come out to see you in Arizona just after you moved when you invited me. You'd found a golf course you liked. A heart surgeon who might help. I should have told your mother I was going and she could come or not come, but as you know, I didn't. I'd heard your unspoken wish for your father when you asked me to visit and I pretended that I didn't. You wanted me to know where you were. You wanted me to know you were safe.

Your mother was in the kitchen opening a can of fig preserves. She'd been trying to open that can our whole conversation. "We're not going," she said when I hung up, and her back straightened with resolve. "He wanted to leave. He's left."

She was a proud woman, your mother. She thought she could out-wait you. She thought you'd come home and then she could welcome you back, her special prodigal son. But you never did, and here we are on opposite sides of the bridge, nothing but hazy signals flashing in the distance.

Raven's Mother

I started tipping a bit of the Old Crow, but that weren't no one's business but my own. I wasn't hurting no one. I went to church every Sunday. I dressed up right, wore my hat, and sat in our pew. There weren't nobody going to say I didn't do what I was expected to do. I didn't ever get drunk; drunk's for sinners and sailors, and I never been neither, but I do declare, though, the whiskey, it did a thing for me. I guess with some folks they drink it to quiet things down, but for me, it woke things up and when those things were awake I was just better able to get along in my day. When those things were awake I felt like I was a little more living and I won't apologize for it, not to you, not to anyone. God made whiskey like He done made every other thing and whether it's sainted or sinned depends on how you use it. I'm right in my heart, y'all gonna talk if y'all gonna talk.

After your daddy died, there was too much quiet. For a man who never had nary a thing to say, it was surprising how much more quiet it was after he crossed. Too much quiet makes a woman get to thinking and when I got to thinking I heard too many folks long gone swirling about my brain like an undertow.

At first I had a finger at sundown on the porch, sipping slow while the creek turned red. Then I splashed a finger in my morning juice while the creek turned gold. I drank it from those tiny glasses with the big oranges on them we got with our Greenbax Stamps from the Piggly Wiggly. Sometimes when I hold one, I see your palm wrapped around it, your upper lip dotted with pulp.

How could I go away to no old folks' home, son? How would you find me there?

Raven

Everything is crashing in on me from sea to sea I never thought my life would span an alphabet of states would take me farther when I'd only meant to be nearer only meant to be clearer in my own attacked heartline. I grow confused here now where once was comfort is chatter-chat-chatter but not my chatter someone else's many else's and the voices are so foreign yet so dear. I thought I was alone I was left bereft to perch and to watch my child my blood I was left to atone my bones this clacking sound to wander aimless in this velvet underground and now I hear some ghost voice whispering what I've most desired to know.

Mother, you remembered me?

Raven's Mother

I wore red lipstick and my strand of real pearls every day until my last. Even when the red bled into the folds of my lips, even when the flesh on my neck stretched and dotted, I dressed right. Sometimes I put on my stockings and my face and just sat in the front room waiting for visitors to come. Do you remember how many people used to come visit us? Not since you had the polio—that was the last time the visiting was so quiet. No one came to our house because we'd been cursed somehow. God had disapproved of something and had chosen you to let us know. Folks were afraid they'd catch it. Afraid they'd become us. The same thing happened after your daddy died, even though just about all of us were getting ready to meet Jesus. People didn't come, or when they did, they wouldn't set a spell, wouldn't let me bring the sweet tea, wouldn't let me talk. It's odd how people closest to death grow more afraid of it. I was not afraid of death, son. I summoned it.

I'll bet you didn't know that was possible, but it is, and it happens more often than you'd recognize. After a time, I didn't miss the visitors right much because I had plenty of others to talk to and I didn't have to pretend like they didn't exist. I made the mistake once of telling your sister that I was speaking with your daddy every evening and that was when she commenced to looking to put me in a home. I spent a fair amount of energy talking to your daddy, talking to you, and I didn't have patience for nobody who thought it weren't real. We couldn't see your polio when it creeped into our house, but nobody dared tell us that weren't real. Invisibility doesn't mean something ain't the truth.

After a time, I laid out food for you both and we three'd set at that pine table and I'd hear the clinking of your forks on the china and gurgles of your bellies as they settled and I may have gained a right good amount of weight in those years but it was just from having so many meals together—so many meals filled with us. Some evenings we'd eat a whole chicken and I'd pull the wishbone greasy between my fingers and I'd wish for you to stay another day and when I'd open my eyes, there you'd be, just shimmering white with the glory of God.

I had rituals. Some nights I'd sleep in your room, just lay me down on that quilt Aunt Lena Mae made for you, and stare up at the ceiling. The room had a view of the creek because we knocked down the wall when we added on that outdoor pantry. Didn't have no creek view when it was yours, and I'm sorry for that. I'd try to imagine what it might've been like for you to go to bed a running, jumping boy and wake up unable to move from your neck down, but I'd fall short. I suppose I could be faulted for not giving enough empathy to you then, son, but I had no room for empathy. I had to save you. I had to make you want to walk, want to live, and all I knew to give fire to a body to do the impossible was rage.

There. I said that word. Is that what you were waiting for? Now it can hang between us like a dirty sheet. Yes. I stoked your rage. I tried to make you furious and even now in this day wherever it is that I am I will not apologize for it. Seems like this here middle place is where I'm supposed to do all sorts of apologizing, but I won't have none of it. I did what I did with intention and to apologize for it—well, that would be the bigger sin.

Your rage made you live, son, and that came straight from your mother. Don't you forget it. The very thing you ran from in me I planted inside you to make sure you grew.

Raven

You expect me to let go of the things you said the way you left me all but dead ashamed of me your boy who once was strong but then fell sick and made you look like you were weak and out of favor with your precious God. You were the one who told me I had sinned told me I was sin incarnate stamped by God as a message to the rest of all the world. My limp became my mark of Cain everything I did earned your disdain and so I had no choice but to pack up all my life and go away.

And by the way you didn't leave me all but dead you left me when I was truly dead and when they laid me down there was not one person from my life before my wife. I'm supposed to let all of that just go? Where is Daddy?

Me

Hello?

15

I search for you in the eyes of my childhood best friend's father. He's one of the few people still alive who knew you, but he won't be living long. His knuckles sprout short white hairs. He is unreachable now, his mind folded in on itself, hospital corners of locked memories. If I visit my childhood best friend's father, I will be able to say goodbye to you again. I will be able to look into eyes that once looked into yours, and no matter that he has moved into liminal space, he once occupied a backyard with you that smelled of charcoal briquettes and steak.

The last time I see him is in 2012. He leans on my rental car window's edge, eyes still playful, and says: "I think of your daddy every day."

I catch those words in a net and stick pins in them and mount them to my wall.

I love you, I want to say to my friend's father but don't. I want to hold his hand, which once shook yours, though 7 x 4 + 2 years of skin cells have dissolved since then.

He has died now. Maybe he is with you. Maybe you both are working on the Ford's engine again. Maybe you are remembering me, remembering my childhood best friend.

My friend and I are now on the shadow side of fifty, but there's a backyard where we're always ten, playing out past dark and catching fireflies in mason jars, waiting for your call.

"Girls! Come inside!"

But no voice remains.

Raven's Mother

I did not attend your funeral. How could I? Everything about it was wrong. It was in the wrong state with the wrong people in the wrong dirt. But that weren't what was most wrong with it. What was most wrong with it was you being dead, and if I went to watch them put you in that desert then I'd have to know there weren't no way you'd be coming back to me—to us—to home, and I couldn't do that. That's another thing I won't apologize for—being unwilling to say you're dead. And it turned out I didn't need to because I brought you right back into the house anyway and we were able to carry on like we used to and ever' once in a while we'd laugh.

Raven

That wasn't me I see I see from sea to shining sea that thing you talked to in your house once Daddy died it was not me.

Me

Am I talking to you? Or are you not you?

Raven

_____.

Me

Oh God.

Raven's Mother

Of course it was you. Who knows you better than your mother? You left your footprints in my belly. No one else on earth can say that.

Raven

Mother.

Raven's Mother

Son.

Raven's Father

Son.

Raven

Dad?

Me

Dad?

Raven

It was not me could not be me when I died I have been wandering perching watching I have been flying in this maze this haze of velvet dark while parts of me flew into other places leaving traces of who I thought I was scattered in some hell that has no name. You conjured up someone forsaken spent your evenings undertaking all the conversations you did not dare have when I was living, but there can be no mistaking the only one in that kitchen was you. And there was the me that you made up the husband you made up to keep you company on all those days that stretched beyond our lives but those ghosts that you called in were nothing but figments of your cracked apart heart nothing but wraiths to decorate your empty walls.

Raven's Mother

I saw you, son, each morning and each night. I made you scrambled eggs and biscuits and gravy and I turned the radio on so you could hear the weather and the tides. You always liked to listen to the tide forecast.

Raven

I liked to listen to baseball.

Raven's Mother

You said the tide forecast helped you remember that everything changes.

Raven

I never said anything like that.

Raven's Mother

You said the tides reminded you of Jesus.

Raven

I never did.

Raven's Mother

If I recollect right, it was just a day or two after you died that you came back to us. Your daughter called your sister to tell us about it. No one bothered to call us, your parents. I never much liked your wife, but that's not news. I made that pretty clear over all the years she took you from me.

I like to think you arrived with your final letter. When the postman lifted that letter from his bag and slipped it in our mailbox at the end of the long drive, I like to think he deposited you in that metal box as well (and I tried to forget that you were by then already in a metal box, already under the ground). I imagine you curled up inside the folds of the envelope, dated two days before you died, arriving to us four days afterwards on the day of your funeral. I imagine you let a part of yourself slip into that letter, some part of you that knew you were just about to go, some part of you that wanted to be carried on back home.

It was your daddy who brought in the letter. I asked him, I

said, "Daddy, you look like you saw a ghost!" And I was trying to make a bit of a joke because we all were right unsure what to be doing with ourselves now that you'd died.

Your daddy hadn't been to bed since the news. He just went outside and wandered, leaving me in the house all alone, but then he brought you in, signed, sealed, delivered like that Elvis sinning song said, and he was shaking, your daddy was, shaking with that little piece of paper. He set your letter on the dining room table and we both stared at it a good while, neither one of us wanting to break it open, neither one of us wanting to be the one to slice the seal your tongue made. Finally, I picked it up and I traced our names on the envelope, my finger slipping into the grooves the pen made—your pen made—and I felt my fingerprints merging with yours and it felt electric.

Your ghost came into the house then.

My fingerprints woke him up, like rubbing some genie's lamp and hoping against all good sense that you'd get your wish granted. Your daddy felt it too. He startled some and when I looked at him, I saw how red his eyes had gotten—all those days with no sleep just wandering in the field lost like Job—and us still having to get us presentable for the funeral we were hosting for you here at home. I felt suddenly full of all kinds of energy and excitement because you'd chosen to be with us on the day of your burial, not out in that desert with all that sun and wrong dirt.

We didn't open that letter. Not for several weeks. We propped it up on the table in the napkin holder and treated it like a centerpiece.

But of course when we looked at it from a certain angle, that envelope looked just like a tombstone etched with all our names.

Me

I'm losing control of this narrative. This was supposed to be my story. This was supposed to be about Dad and me and my lifelong story of holding on to grief and now I see there were no players in that script but me. Dad was mine to hold, mine to mine, mine to analyze and dramatize. Mine. But other characters had other ideas, other claims, other commitments. Including Dad.

16

I don't know what I expected would happen if I let all the ghosts out to play on their own velvet black stage.

I don't know why I'm surprised that the dead have their own words.

Agendas.

Grievances.

I've never been very good at writing by outline—at plotting the inciting incident between pages thirty and forty, the climax by page 210, and the non-sentimental but nonetheless satisfyingly transformative ending at an easily digestible length of 270 pages. I took the classes on how to create this well-traveled map. I teach these classes. But still, story refuses to comply.

I don't know why this surprises me.

I, too, refuse to comply.

Raven

I am no one.

Me

I am a figment of my own imagination.

Raven's Mother

You came to us in an envelope and we put you on the table.

Raven's Father

I carried you in from the mailbox like I carried you back from the hospital after your polio. I ate breakfast with you and then took you out to the cornfields so we could talk.

Me

I carried you back from the hospital on the day you died and I put you in my belly and then you turned into a tumor. My yearning for you transmogrified into cells that devoured themselves, cells that were myopic in their cannibalism.

Raven

I did none of these things.

Me

I built you like a character in a novel and I fell asleep to your whispers at night.

Raven's Mother

I gained thirty pounds eating three meals a day with you.

Raven's Father

I knelt in the sand in the field and pretended to tend to the vegetables, but I drew pictures in the dirt, remembering holding your fingers to help you write your name. My name. Our name. Glenn.

Raven

I entered this place this space and I have seen from sea to sea all the fragments I could be.

Raven's Mother

It started with just a splash of whiskey at night.

Raven's Father

Just for a few days, I thought I'd walk the fields with you for just a few days and then I'd let you go.

Me

I would keep you safe inside of me. When you died, I opened my mouth and inhaled your ghost.

Raven's Mother

That splash of whiskey opened up the world and I could hear you clearer so I dropped in a splash or two more.

Raven's Father

All I could think about was getting back outside to the field with you. I went back to the house only to eat, only to wash. Some nights I slept under stars between the butter beans and tomatoes. If I pressed my ear to the soil, I could hear the rumbling of the sea just a mile away. If I dug a hole deep enough, I knew I could find you in that desert grave, so I started to tunnel and the work felt good in my bones and under moonlight it all made sense. In sunlight, I covered the hole with planks and tried to shake the sand from my feet.

Me

The week they laid your stone in the desert dirt, I went to the cemetery at sunset with a pillow and blanket and I curled up on top of the new grass sprouting over your belly and I slept uninterrupted for the first time since you'd died.

When you came to me in the hospital after my surgery, I clicked the morphine button to make sure you'd stay and once the morphine left and you began to speak in fragments hopping on your shortened leg, squawking in the window and perching on the bedpost, I was so relieved. You came back. You came back. You came back.

Raven

I did not.

Me

_____.

Raven's Father

You came back to the field.

Raven

I did not.

Raven's Mother

You came back to the house.

Raven

I did not.

Me

You came to my backyard.

Raven

I did not.

Me

_____!

Raven

I'm not me you see you see I'm your wish for me please, daughter, see from sea to sea these things are not the same.

Me

But you came back.

Raven

_____.

17.

I DON'T WANT TO LET YOU GO.

IF I TELL YOU WHAT I'VE HIDDEN, THEN YOU'LL GO.

WHO AM I TALKING TO ANYWAY?

I DON'T REMEMBER YOU AT ALL.

I ONLY REMEMBER THE STORIES I WROTE.

Raven's Father

When you contracted polio, we struggled. Your mother said it was because you displeased God and that you needed to confess. I agreed with her because by that point all I knew to do was agree with her, but it couldn't be that. It had to be random. What child could have done something so wrong? I don't believe in fate. I don't believe our lives have been predetermined. It would be easier if I did believe it, easier if causality fell like rain.

God is supposed to be generous, but God is also malicious and vindictive. He is supposed to love us, but he pulls that love away when we don't do as he desires. We are supposed to rejoice in his love, fall on our knees to earn it, and then flagellate ourselves when something goes awry—when a leg goes to sleep and doesn't wake up, when a heart attacks itself.

The preachers tell us we desire to feast with God in heaven, but I don't know that I do. I don't know that I want to shake the right hand of the thing responsible for your polio, your heart. I don't know what to make of this world, and I know you're thinking I'm a hypocrite for sitting in the pew next to your mother for all those years, but I know this: the day polio came was the day God left.

When I died, I looked for you, son, but I didn't see you. When your mother died, I didn't see her. Maybe I'm not where I think I am, but every day I keep going, hoping for a glimpse of life.

Some mornings, when the sun is just cracking across the sky, I can see all of it, from sea to sea, I see, and some mornings there is nothing but dark.

Raven

Daddy?

Raven's Father

Son, I have regrets, but none as great as not going to Arizona for your funeral. Maybe that is why I am here in the somewhere-dark. Maybe that is why I can't find you or your mother or my own mother and father, my own sisters and brothers.

I feel sometimes like I'm in a hall cloaked in black velvet. I can see shapes of doorknobs and window ledges, but I can't get to them. Sometimes I hear bits of conversations or bars of music, like someone is tuning a radio dial, but it never lasts long enough for me to rest with it. I hadn't thought how much pleasure a person gets from listening to a whole piece of music until all I could hear were parts.

I'm thinking maybe that's a metaphor for how a life works, son. I know it's unlikely that I'd talk in metaphors, seeing as high school was as far as I got and my poetry came from the earth, from the way the corn and the squash and the okra grew, rather than from the fine print pages of books. But what I'm wondering now that I have this time to wander is whether each of us only hears a few measures from the lives of those around us, and then from what we hear we make up the whole piece of music, but that piece of music is really about us and not at all about the bits we overheard. And then of course those bits are also just composed of the snippets those folks were hearing too and I guess I don't know where all this ends. Where there is one source for a story. One source for a life.

What I'm thinking is different here is that I know I'm only hearing paragraphs. When I was on the earth, I thought I heard the story. I feel like I can hear you now, but when I try to dial it in, it turns to static.

My granddaughter called your sister when you died and she came over and told us. Your mother, well, she took it in with silence and then closed herself in the bedroom leaving me and your sister standing on the porch looking out at that creek, and I remember thinking how odd it was that I could see you running along the pier and leaping into the water. I saw you running at the age you were before the polio ate your leg and I had to stop myself from walking out to join you, from leaping into the waterway, from finding the mouth of the alligator who'd lived there longer than we had.

Your wife told your sister not to come to Arizona. She was handling it; she was fine, and we knew she would be but it hurt us to be shut away from you. My granddaughter, she thinks we didn't come because it was too expensive to fly and that was what your mother said, but that was just a sentence from the story. We never knew how to relate to your wife. She never knew how to relate to us. And so we held a service for you in our house in the South on the same day of your funeral in the West. We talked about you and we laughed a little and we prayed a lot because your mother and your sister were worried about your soul.

Son, you should know I was never worried about your soul. I knew it was perfect.

But we should have been there to see you put into the desert ground, into earth that did not bear you, did not hold centuries of ancestor bones. We should have stood under that sun that never had cloud cover, that glaring penetrating desert sun, and worn our hats for you. We should have brought our bones to yours. I didn't realize how much we all would need that.

Is that why we can't find each other, son? What if we're walking down parallel velveted hallways, still hearing only fragments of each other's lives? What if hell is not at all what we were taught but rather this disconnected maze where we just wander, reaching for each other, pressing our skeletons against the soft fabric walls, leaving imprints?

I was here. I am here. I will be here.

Where were you? Where are you? Where will you be?

The hand-bone connected to the heart-bone. Dance with me, son. My bones ache for yours.

Raven's Mother

I insisted on your funeral at our house, son. Your wife told us

150

not to come, or maybe she said she was fine and I took that to mean we would not need to get on that plane and go to that desert and see you buried in the dirt. I honestly can't remember anymore. I know I didn't want to go. If we went we'd have to see you put in the ground, and we spent all we had of our lives, son, to make sure you stayed alive. If we went it would be real. So the preacher came over, and your sister came over, and all the folks who knew you when you were the March of Dimes poster boy for polio who were still living came over, and we had us a service. We sang the songs you would have wanted, the old spirituals, not the minor-keyed Lutheran songs of your wife. We laughed a little and we prayed a lot but most of all, we had a gathering without your body so it was more like you were away on a trip, or maybe like you were someone we had all dreamed together, but no matter, it was possible to believe you weren't gone. And that was the most important thing.

We were sure taken aback when your last letter arrived a few days later. Then it took some powerful forces of energy to keep you living, but your daddy and me, we were strong enough to do that. We were strong enough to hold you here.

I held everything. Folks called me a hoarder, called me stingy, but I didn't care. I knew what it felt like to have everything gone, and by everything I mean you, son. I mean all the dreams we had for you taken that morning polio snuck into our house. I hadn't held you tight enough. I'd let you go into the creek, or visit a friend, or eat in the cafeteria. I'd let you go and polio took you and I could not ever let anything go again.

I gathered dresses and shoes. Ketchup and mustard packets. Napkins. Tupperware. Wrapping paper. Wax paper. Preserves. I stuffed them under the beds and into the closets. I filled the vanity drawers and the silverware drawers and the pantry shelves. If there was a space, I put something in it. I forgot about a lot of what I put in the spaces, but that was never the point—the stuff wasn't what I needed. I needed to weigh myself down. I needed to be sure everything we might want was always there, even if it rotted before I found it again. I thought storing up would save us, and whenever anyone tried to take anything from me, I held even tighter. I'd learned what happens when a mother lets go, and I would never let another thing slip through my fingers.

Raven

Hello?

Me

Where are we? I smell salt and red clay mud and humid damp.

Raven

Daddy?

Raven's Mother

Son?

Raven's Father

Son, I need to find your bones.

When we opened your last letter, you had already been dead two days. You wrote about fatigue and irrelevance. Laraine was coming for lunch, you said, but you didn't know what you had to offer her anymore. You had bought your plane ticket for the October Homecoming at Masonboro Baptist as you'd done most years since you moved West, even though you left the church years before. Your mother prayed. Your sister prayed. I understood why you walked away, but I stayed silent while you struggled with the God we'd given you. I was afraid of my own fight with Him, afraid if I gave a breath to it, it would consume me.

It did anyway, son. After you'd gone.

You were the polio boy who lived. Our own March of Dimes miracle story, and we old ones, the ones who were young when you were quarantined, remembered waiting in the hospital lobby while so many of our children went limp and died. We projected a lot of our hope into you, the one who lived, the one who walked, the one who raged, and we thought you'd always be ours. We thought you'd always return home to the creek and the sand and the sea. We grew you like we grew our corn and butter beans. We grew you like pine: fragrant, soft. We grew you like hickory with deep, strong roots.

I didn't yet understand that God was random.

After your polio, the muscles in your right leg stopped holding up your bones and your body fell into a pile of flesh, your spirit the only fuel left, and, son, we had never seen anything like it. Our preacher prayed over you and you grew stronger and you showed us all that God was great.

Raven

Stop it stop it stop I say you pray they prayed my pain away they

153

prayed not that I get better they put conditions on it made it so I was not enough. Would never be enough. They said they said their palms upon my head they said, "Lord if this child will grow up to serve you, please spare his life. If not please spare another."

And then they left me in the iron bed their fire and brimstone on my head and you took from that that God was great but that was not what made me take that first step out of bed that first scream that echoed sea to sea what made me do those things was me not God was me and my response to judgment on my bones was to take their fire and conspire to get far away and fast away until the dust of home was nothing but the smoke I passed across my lips with every exclamation point and question mark my home turned into toxic air.

Raven's Father

Son, is that you?

Raven

_____!

Raven's Father

Son, I lived for two and a half years after you died.

I put food in my body, water on my lips, my feet in the fields where we had talked those days after you had your heart attack and were looking for home. I listened for you in the copperheads that wove around the garden, looked for your footprints on the alligator's submerged head, waited on the porch until the frogs no longer sang.

When I sank into the earth at Masonboro Baptist Church with all the rest of our ancestors—row upon row upon row of Herrings under moss and branch—I could not rest. The divot on my skull looked for your elbow. My fingers sought your thumb, my feet your palms and before too long I began to walk, not unlike you did after you left your iron lung. One toe pushed against the mud from underneath, one leg cracked the surface, then the next. My arms, my spine soon followed, my divoted skull the last to pop above the ground, and when I wandered around the tiles of tombstones, my own name, Glenn, shimmered seeking your own name, Glenn.

Son, don't you know we named you after me so we could find you? A "junior" is a rope between us.

When you were born, your bones fit in our arms. The divot of your skull rested in the bend of my elbow, the whole of your feet in my palms, your spine on my forearm, your fingers around my thumb. When you stretched out of our reach, we watched you running, climbing, jumping, and God was good then. God is gone now. I could not rest with all the Herrings' bones decaying without yours. My coffin was a cage and I snapped my knees back into place and started walking toward the West, toward sea and salt and sand. My eye sockets caught the wind, my jaw clattered in the rain, but I kept moving, following the calling of your bones.

I wanted to go to you when you were still living but I held my tongue, kept the peace, picked my battles—any one of those ridiculous metaphors. I didn't fight hard enough for you, but I'll tell you something you might not know. When you took your family West away from us, she cried and tried to make you stay by guilting you about all we'd done for you. You took that as one more trick, one more manipulation, and it was, but under all that, son, she couldn't see a world for herself without you in it. She simply could not let you go so she pushed you away instead.

I think your daughter might know a thing or two about that pattern. She could not let you go so she pushed everything else away.

We have to find each other again, son, so we can help her do what we could not. Please wait for me. I am on my way.

Raven

I died before you and no one was there to meet me greet me no one had gone before who knew me I wandered so long I wandered wondered where you were where were you where were you where were you?

Me

Daddy, where were you?

Raven's Father

Son, where are you?

Raven

I went back to the house on the creek where I ran and I jumped and I swam and I went to the barn where the chickens were sent to the barn where we put down my bird dog my bird dog I thought I would see him again.

Wilbur.

I thought I would see him again.

I saw I saw I saw from sea to sea and I thought that you

would come for me you and Mother I thought you would come to the desert to bury my bones that had fit in the crooks of your arms but you didn't you didn't and when I went into the dirt none of my birth people were there to send me home.

Caw! Caw! Caw! I returned to North Carolina for Homecoming every year and to my Homegoing you did not did not go.

Raven's Father

Do I hear you, son, or do I just long to? So long have I been walking. I didn't know a body could walk so long and get no-where.

Raven

Daddy, I needed you.

Me

Daddy, I needed you.

Raven

I remember I remember I remember when I was eight my legs had died and I lay with other children dead in rows of iron beds just waiting for the crows to perch upon their heads and take them.

I lay behind the quarantine door no one could touch me I was poison I was both dying and death but, Daddy, I was just a boy.

I heard I heard I heard the doctor say to you there was nothing more to do that you should get a wheelchair build a ramp and take me home and you said no no no you would not do that would not take me back like that you would wait and you would watch and you would fight for me to walk to live. The doctor shook his head and said to you he's almost dead and you said almost isn't dead almost is living still and I heard you in my iron bed I heard you tell the doctor no you are not right and so when night returned I fell into my bones and built a raging fire all-consuming with desire to walk myself back to our creek our soil our soul.

And walk I did when all they said was no they all said no except for you for you and me and together we started over crawling falling walking never running not again not running but together we walked me back alive.

Caw! Caw! I have been walking a long time here in the dark.

Raven's Father

I have been walking a long time in the dark.

Me

I told the doctors no.

Raven

Tell me.

Me

I have to tell it in second person. I still can't fit my I into my body.

Raven

Tell it how you need to tell it
telling it will slip it into a different chapter
telling it will kick it out of its groove and into the sky.
I float. I fly.
I will snatch your story in my beak my weak leg will hold it hold it hold it and when your ending comes I will let us both down softly.

19

In the waiting room at the oncologist's office, the light is the sour yellow of old grade school classrooms. The industrial carpet once held a pattern of diamonds, but now is a flattened copper sheet. Hospice brochures poke up from plastic dispensers, inkjetted wildflowers in dead soil. The people sitting near you are also yellow—their skin, their eyes, their teeth. They are in wheelchairs or they are in walkers or they are alone, shaking.

You sit with them, not shaking, your decision already made, though your calves are sprouting wings, readying for flight. The plastic orange chair you sit on conveys disposability, anonymity—the chairs of rural airports and the DMV. Chairs that are easy to clean from unexpected fluids. There is no art on the beige walls. You whisper to your husband, "I am not doing this," and he says wait, let's hear what they have to say—or maybe he says nothing, just holds your hand. He has had a rough month too, standing by while you were disemboweled by a giant robot named Eva in a hospital one hundred miles away from your mountain home.

You made the appointment with this oncologist. You are one to keep appointments because you cannot bear to disappoint. But you watch the people signing in and then disappearing—chemotherapy to the left, radiation to the right—and you know that here in the waiting room, the only place the two roads converge, will be the only point you will have the freedom to make the decision you think you have made. But it isn't about making the decision. You know this. It is about *stating* the decision and that is another thing entirely. If you speak it out loud, you will disappoint. You will not be the good girl. You will become non-compliant. You cannot bear to disappoint.

But let's back up because your decision was so clear you dismissed it as you have done so many times before.

But let's reconstruct anyway. Let's back it up some more.

What you know:

Your imagination is wild and unpredictable.

You can convince yourself of any spooky thing.

You can conjure images and trick yourself into believing they are real or not real.

You cannot trust yourself because of this.

The first thing you notice when you drive into the parking lot is the sign that reads *No Handicapped Parking Available.* This is an oncology practice. Surely there are people who need these spaces. But you don't, at least not yet, and so you prepare to enter the sliding double doors, but she is blocking your way—a flash, a flashback, a flash forward. She is crouched on the other side of the silver threshold wearing her favorite red dress and red Stride-Rite leather sandals. She is staring up at you, and if you put your foot down, you'll step right through her. You haven't seen her in so long—this you, eight years old, right before everything changed for her. Before her dad had his first heart attack, before the cross-country move that left half her heart in North Carolina, before her abusive fiancé, before the weight loss and the weight gain and the weight loss. Forty years before the cancer. But there you are, looking down at you looking up at you, her eight-year-old hand raised *stop!*

In the seven weeks since your surgery, your mind has found its own way to pass the time. Conjuring old selves is a favorite and familiar activity. But you're not lying in bed now while everyone else is at work. You're not listening to another episode of *Longmire* or *NCIS* because you can't bear the silence but also can't concentrate enough to watch anything of substance. You've already gone down the Google-hell of survival rates, treatment options, recommendations, and survivor forum horror stories. You think you know what the oncologist will say, so you are unprepared for the pop up of your Red-Riding-Hood girl-self on the other side of the sliding double doors.

She keeps her hand up like she is directing traffic, and when it's apparent you're going inside the building anyway (you have an appointment; you hate to disappoint), she screams, "Let me do it myself!" No one else sees her of course, and you can't disrupt the flow of traffic: the Dial-A-Ride drivers help the wheelchaired folks in and out of the office, and the ones who can walk on their own emerge from the left hallway and the right hallway, gazing far away. Everyone knows you can't stop at a crossroad. You mustn't snarl traffic, take up space, be seen. Not wanting to disrupt, you step around her. Your husband doesn't see her either, but she follows you both inside onto the flat copper carpet and sits at your feet between the shiny legs of the orange plastic chairs. She massages your calves, helping your wings sprout from the muscle, pressing each feather out, finger by finger. She is blowing her breath into them, whirling them into their beat.

You are called back. Left side. Chemotherapy side, but she won't let go of you. She holds tight to your legs, her own feet dragging ruts in the carpet. You want to make a good impression (you hate to disappoint). They (just who is *they* anyway?) tell you that you need an oncologist now, even though the surgeon took it all out and it didn't travel to other organs and it didn't breach the colon wall. Still, you are marked now. You have *the diagnosis*. But you reject the diagnosis and you don't know how to explain—yes, of course you accept you had a tumor. You saw the pictures. But you reject the stories that come with that label. There is a ready-written narrative for you now and all you have to do is walk down the right path or the left path and the ending becomes the cliché.

You fight the chapters that have been flung at you since *the diagnosis*. The words that circle round your head—flapping consonants and vampire-vowels searching for your jugular. You are not a cancer patient, nor a cancer survivor. Rather, you are a woman who had a malignant growth in her colon and now you don't. And so now you will not:

- dissolve under the weight of the words that accompany *the diagnosis*

- walk down the left path or the right path

161

- become brittle

- turn gray

You reject them all, though you will listen to the oncologist (you hate to disappoint), because you are a good girl and a good student and you respect authority and the doctors know the language of *the diagnosis* and if you treat people with respect they will respect you back, except when they don't. You will listen because you have made lists and they will save you.

Your eight-year-old red-sandaled self hasn't yet learned her world operates on its own terms, not hers. She runs her tiny fingers through the wings she birthed from your calves, priming each white feather, stroking its spine, whispering into its root. Your hamstrings are taut with the surprising weight of the wings. She tenses when the doctor enters. He doesn't make eye contact with you, and when he opens your file, it is clear he never looked it over, even though you (good girl, good student, good patient) were told to send everything a week before the appointment so he could prepare. He skims the seven-page surgical report in less time than it takes you to brush your teeth.

He tells your husband—not you, he never looks at you—that you need six weeks of chemotherapy and six weeks of radiation and we can start today. Oh, wait, what is your insurance? Ah. Okay. Yes. We can start right away and we should get a PET scan just in case. The doctor still has not spoken to you and you have lost your voice. His dismissal makes you feel you have already failed as a patient (you are good student; you do not disappoint). If you interrupt the doctor, if you raise your voice, you'll break the rules and become a bad girl, bad student, bad patient.

"What took you so long to come see me?" he finally says to you.

You open your mouth. Your head is screaming. Long? You were in surgery seven weeks ago. You still can't control your bowels, and your surgeon told you to follow up in three months with an oncologist so you are fucking early (you are always fucking early), but you don't say any of that, your only betrayal your lips, gaping open and closed like a beached fish. You researched stage 2 colon cancer before the appointment and learned that adjuvant treatment (another new word pair) is controversial at this stage because the risks outweigh the benefits from a successful surgery. But you are not a doctor, as has become painfully obvious these past two months.

"Why?" is all you can squeak out and he tells you that the explanation for the nuclear options of chemotherapy and radiation would be Greek to you. *Try me*, you should have said. You are not an MD, but you have two masters' degrees and you're actually pretty darn proficient in Latin, so *bring it*, but you don't say that either. You are mute. Muted. He has muted you. Your colors drain into the beige walls.

"T3!" he finally says, frustrated because you have not acquiesced. "Your tumor is T3!" He points at a drawing of the colon and then tosses the book of illustrations on the table with a thud. Your husband has also been muted. Neither of you like to disappoint.

Your wings have gone still, the girl's hands knead your ankles, your calves. She blows her new warm breath back on the feathers until they flutter. "What if we don't do anything more now?" you ask. "How can we monitor it?"

"You can take the chemo as a pill now or you can get a port later when it comes back," he says and looks at his watch.

Your rage is iron in your lungs, but it has clamped your tongue. *You don't know me*, you shriek in your head. *I will not be back here.* But you are silent. Tears are hot at the backs of your eyes but you won't let them fall. You won't let this man see one living thing from your heart.

He is exasperated. You are non-compliant. "I can see you don't understand," he says, but not in the way a teacher who is wanting to help you understand would speak. He sees you don't understand in the way that proves you are an idiot. He is the smart one in his poorly lit office with the two paths and the prescriptioned ending. He stands and waves you both away. "Go ahead. Get a second opinion."

I can do this myself! she shouts from the floor. Your eight-year-old self has no iron in her lungs. She has no shame tears at the edges of her eyes (you have already failed; you have become ill; you are a weak one in the herd). You and your husband stand, erased and dismissed. You are shaking but she, she is solid, child's hands on your ankles, a squeeze and a pinch. *Go.* She does not falter. She does not need to please or impress. The doctor doesn't offer his hand, just opens the door. You grab your notebook where you had intended to make notes, ask questions, build a relationship with this man, but the pages remain empty. It was all Greek to you.

When you stand, the wings spread, expanding to fit the whole office. She holds your hand. The iron corset unclasps from your tongue, clink, clink, and it swells to fill your mouth. You choke, spit, gasp, and exit the room. Other patients are down the hall sitting in large brown chairs, clear liquid pouring into ports. *This is real, Laraine. Don't be so cocky. You are not a doctor. You are not an oncologist. You are unqualified to second guess a doctor.* At the front desk, you sign out and then collapse in the car. "It's not just me, right?" you ask your husband. "He was awful."

"He was awful," he says.

Go, she says. So clear. She is this many fingers—one hand plus three. *Let me,* she says. *We can put ourselves back together.* The wings are golden in the late morning yellow. They haven't contracted in the car. You realize you can stretch them out. *Don't let go of me.*

"I'm not doing chemo or radiation," you tell your husband, and you realize this is what you knew before you met the oncologist. You will be meeting with a different doctor for the first time in just one hour. One who:

- specializes in integrative cancer treatments
- spends an hour and a half with you
- knows your name
- answers your questions
- asks how your emotions are
- speaks directly to you

- talks to you about diet and other options
- tells you yes, there are many things we can do
- tells you no, chemotherapy is not necessary right now

But you don't know this yet, in the front seat holding her hand, feeling your wings shivering in the light. Even though this language is new to you—*T3, adenocarcinoma, survival rates, prognosis, malignancy, margins, nodes*—you will not become your diagnosis, will not be defined by words. You will remain autonomous, will unlock your tongue after forty years of silencing it, and breathe air into your rusted lungs, and this will be the first time that you wonder whose skin you have worn and why and when you stopped wearing red leather shoes with fancy brass buckles beneath calves that bore the wings of angels.

Raven

Polio was coming back I couldn't say I didn't say I couldn't name its name but it re-entered just the same. I thought it had left me after feeding on my muscles tendons nerves I thought that I deserved at least this certainty—that what had gone to sleep would not wake up but that is not the way it worked it snuck around my body until it found the perfect spot to settle in begin again take the last bit of freedom I had found.

Me

What if cancer comes back?

Raven

That's the dance the chance you take when you open up your life. I cannot tell you if it will or if it won't I can only tell you if you don't make this time in between the cancer and whatever's next you will be prisoner twice will splice your ending before it has been written.

Me

At night I sometimes hear it feeding.

Raven

Everything must eat.

Me

Even disease.

Raven

Even that.

Me

How did you make peace with your body?

Raven

I had trouble sleeping keeping my mind behind my heart I'd start to panic bubble thought up into thought until my lungs began to choke and I woke up sweating fraught with terror. I did this until I died but I died just the same do you see do you see?

20

The terrified young nurse chases me down the hospital hall. "Where are you going?"

I am pulling my IV drip beside me down the wide carpeted walkway. My catheter had been removed earlier in the day, and as soon as I realized I was no longer tethered to something I couldn't figure out how to unhook, I knew I had to make my move. Days ago, I ditched the electric compression socks that were supposed to prevent the blood clots that could form as a result of remaining in bed for too long. Every few seconds they contracted, squeezing my calves and ankles. They felt like leg irons to me. The socks were hot and made my feet stick out in front of me, toes up like a corpse, and I was having none of that. If I walked around, then I wouldn't get blood clots. Problem solved. I'd removed my oxygen tubing as well, which I knew would make some red light at the nurses' station flash. Funny how it took less than a minute for a nurse to come after me when I was walking down the hall and over an hour when I politely used the call button to get help to the bathroom.

"You can't be out like this. I can walk with you." She is earnest, her brown eyes pleading with me to please go back to my room. I know she is worried she'd be blamed for losing control of me. I am supposed to be patient and play the part of Patient. Compliant. Non-disruptive. The role is clearly laid out in the script.

"I won't tell on you," I say. "I'm fine."

"It's policy," she says.

"I know." It is also policy to keep the bed at a certain height, but I always raised it back up so it was closer to the air conditioning vent. The lead nurse would lower it with a scowl, and when she left, I would raise it. The bill for this unplanned vacation will be upwards of $200,000. The bed will be where I damn well want it to be.

"I can walk with you if you just give me a minute." Someone is calling her on her walkie-talkie. They are speaking in numbers, part of the secret hospital language. "I've got to go," she says as the page broadcasts on the intercom: *Any cardiologist to OR 6 stat. Any cardiologist to OR 6 stat.* "Just—just be careful."

I smile. I am going off-script.

⌘

Sixteen months after I was released from the hospital, we bury our beloved orange and white ragdoll cat, Buddycat. He had been sick for awhile—lymphoma, or heart failure, or liver failure, or lung cancer. The tests to find out were too expensive, so we watched him, played with him, talked to him, and when he clearly took a turn toward Death, went to the vet where they sedated him while we whispered in his ears and scratched his chin, my tears falling on his fur when the doctor injected the final needle. The vet was kind, the veterinary assistant kinder. The receptionist let me cry at the front desk while I fumbled for my credit card.

We drive to the back of the building to wait for Buddycat to be brought to us in a tiny kitty-casket with a heart drawn in black Sharpie on the top. As we sit in the shade, I make a joke about waiting for our drug score in a back alley, but the joke is just because I am feeling the monster starting to wake up in my belly, right behind where my surgical scars are fading.

I go to the YMCA after he dies and run four miles on the elliptical machine, sweat pooling between my breasts, beats from Queen Latifah's "Ladies First" off my "Essential Feminism" playlist pulsing in my ears. I barely get home before collapsing on my bed, the ugly choke-cry that has been at the back of my throat expelling into the room as a snarl. Euthanasia may or may not be humane. The animal is sedated, so we don't know what he feels or doesn't feel when the second, fatal injection occurs. Every time I authorize a euthanasia procedure for one of my cats, I feel grateful that I can do something to prevent long, drawn out suffering, yet horrified that I can have control over this sacred transition. I'm not supposed to write another's Death story.

But these hot tears are not for Buddycat. Those fell in the morning when he died. By the afternoon, those early tears have worn away the dam that had been holding back the older ones— the ones that cracked at my ribs and climbed up my always-aching shoulder. As the outward signs of my cancer diminish, the inner fingerprints from the experience are beginning to glow in neon red, green, yellow, and as my body grows stronger, my emotional memory is waking up and I am determined not to hold anything back anymore.

Until that afternoon, I had only cried once about the cancer, and that was a week before surgery. I was sitting in an Epsom salt bath listening to Sweet Honey in the Rock and I felt so overwhelmed by the beauty of their voices I couldn't imagine leaving such a sound behind. Would there be sounds such as theirs in death? Right. Death has no soundtrack in the hospital. Death is invisible.

I'd spent much of my thirties in grad school studying grief and death and dying and meditating on impermanence and disintegration, but like with everything else, theory and practice are two different things. Had I really, in spite of graduate training and years of practice, thought illness and death would escape me? Yep. At least until I was in my late nineties and in bed after finishing the last chapter of a perfect book. Isn't that the Judeo-Christian promise of a life well-lived? Isn't that what happened to good people in the stories? See how I internalized the prosperity gospel message even though my parents actively rejected that story? My father's body internalized it. And I internalized him.

I cried for about ten minutes in the bathtub while my husband waited in the bedroom. I had told him that if I ever cried during this mess, he had to let me. He had to keep his distance.

"Can't I hold you?" he'd asked.

"No. Not until I'm done. I can't risk stopping the emotion."

That was true, and what I didn't say was also true: I can't have you hold me because I'll see how my cancer diagnosis is scaring you and I'll try to make you feel better because I want you to feel better but also because it will distract me from what I'm feeling, and I really need to only take care of me. I can't divert my energy for you.

But who can say that mess out loud?

Because I am alone the afternoon Buddycat died, I don't need to take care of anyone else. I don't need to hold back anything *(what else have I held back in my life? How else have I contracted rather than released?)* and as I ride the wave that began in the vet's office, I feel fear—not anger or sadness—and terror.

The terror is dressed in an image of my beeping hospital room and I remember how I pushed and pushed to be out faster than they recommended. How I fought to walk as soon as the anesthesia had left my system. How I wanted to chew solid food when they wanted me to only have bone broth. At the time, I thought I was fighting to heal, and I was, but that afternoon of Buddycat's death I realize I was fighting to get out because I could feel the power of the hospital's machine taking me into its guts. It wanted to keep me forever—a patient, a slave.

The hospital's scribe had my name. My social security number. My date of birth. My insurance card. It also had my diagnostic codes. My pathology reports. My treatment plans. It was making a narrative up about me while I was supposed to be resting, supposed to be following their orders, which were supposed to be about my care but were beginning to feel like something much more sinister. It was turning me into a Character in its Story and the hospital narrative is one in which I could never be the heroine. The hospital always wins. The longer I remained in its setting, the more the hospital and cancer took control of my story, and what was worse, it was writing that story using a language I didn't understand. How could *my* story be written in a foreign tongue?

The hospital was trying to consume me—to ingest

171

me—because it constantly needed new energy sources. When people died there, they must be replaced with new, sick people to ensure a proper return on investment for all the high-tech machinery that glowed in every corner. Once the hospital caught you in its jaws, its teeth tattooed a pre-existing condition on your flesh that would follow you everywhere. If you're caught by the system, you've got a label—a genre—that extends long after you take off the hospital band. You're in the club, and it's a very expensive club, and the dues are paid at the hospital's whim with no pricing negotiation.

(And while you're here in this chapter, the scribe interrupts, would you like to see the statistical probability of your survival? I've embedded it in your narrative underneath every sentence.)

I remembered lying in the semi-dark behind the extra-wide door and feeling the hospital, a living thing, creeping around me. Its language—its codes, its bells, its incredible way of talking around you but never to you—was becoming a little too familiar. I knew when the nursing shift changes were. I knew when to expect my surgeon in the mornings to check on my incisions. It had only been a few days and I had made friends with nurses because allies who can navigate otherworldly settings are useful. I found secret passages in the hallways and wandered the cardiac wing, imagining my father in one of those rooms. Once I learned how to disconnect myself from the machines, I knew where to sneak a cup of coffee. I knew that sneaking forbidden coffee was an important act because it was breaking the protocol of the hospital's narrative. I went out for coffee in my own socks, not their compression socks. They would not compress me. I knew I had to keep disrupting its patterns because its familiarity was beginning to frighten me. Familiarity meant I was *adjusting* to my new world and adjustment meant acceptance, and I would not accept this.

Adaptation: humans' greatest superpower. Even the most adverse conditions can be adapted to. This can help us survive and it can also kill us. I had found a hospital routine—ordering breakfast from the computer, talking to the Slovenian woman who cleaned the room, declining the visiting pastor. I knew to steal a clean gown from the stack they'd leave in the hallway in case they forgot to bring me one. I knew if I wanted a shower, I had to call the nurse as soon as the shift changed or it wouldn't happen until evening. That is, until I disrupted the script and learned how to do it myself, my intubated arm hanging out of the shower stall while I one-handed showered like a boss. They called me feisty. I called myself alive. I walked out of the hospital on my discharge day, refusing the wheelchair ("hospital policy, ma'am"), carrying my green pillow and my things.

I.

Walked.

Out.

But until the afternoon of Buddycat's death, I thought I was pushing against the hospital's rules because I was strong. Brave. Fearless, even. But as I choke up phlegm in my bedroom, I know none of those are the reasons. In my bedroom two hundred miles away from my recovery room, I still feel the tubing in my nostrils. I still see the photographs from Bryce Canyon on the hallway walls.

I was terrified the hospital would capture me, and some part of me knew I had to move as quickly as possible out of its belly before I acclimated too much to its system—before it ate too much of me with its medicines. It wanted to burn me and poison me in the name of healing me and I could feel how easy it would be to let them—how easy it would be to surrender everything—my entire life—to a doctor I met only moments before. How easy it would be to defer to a degree and dismiss my own intuition about what was right for me.

I knew I had a tendency to get cocky—to make decisions rashly—and the choices about how to proceed after surgery were arguably the most important decisions of my life. I was literally betting my life on my gut—that same gut which had momentarily gone offline and formed cancer cells. My gut which had held so much of my grief and my rage that it finally had no choice but to turn on itself. But I knew it would be my gut that would save my life. Within the illness lies the healing. If I didn't trust that in those immediate weeks after surgery, I would lose everything.

As I think of Buddycat's orange and white fluffy head, the panic I had not allowed myself to feel while in the hospital wells up. All that trapped energy crushes against my lungs and throat and has gotten stuck in my body. I am experiencing the animalistic fear of being chased by a predator far larger, more cunning, and more sophisticated than I. After my diagnosis, I had promised myself I would not let anything else get stuck in my body, but I didn't even know this was there. I didn't remember feeling afraid and then pushing it down. I'd simply bypassed the fear, turned it into action, and then held it until I had to euthanize my cat. I'd written a scene for myself without understanding its underlying subtext, and as in any incomplete early draft, the holes in my story are beginning to reveal themselves.

What else do I not remember feeling? What else is impacting my heart, my blood pressure, my cells?

I don't dismiss out of hand the value of Western medicine and its gifts. My surgeon saved my life, and the years of research and millions of dollars that went into developing the daVinci robot who performed the surgery saved my life. A colonoscopy saved my life. I am lucky that the tumor could be removed, lucky that it was found before it had spread outside the colon, lucky that I had insurance and a job I could leave and return to. Lucky, lucky, lucky, lucky. And still terrified. I had to, in a split second after being disemboweled by a machine, discern what treatment was useful and what would be harmful, and as I sat in the veterinarian's exam room with Buddycat and Death, I felt Her hand on my own shoulder again.

"You ran," she said to me not unkindly. "But I'm inside of you."

And of course, She was. Always had been. I was born with Death inside of me, like every other living thing, but being in the hospital woke Her up. By any actuarial chart, I'm on the downturn—middle age only if I live to be 100.

"I've been waiting your whole life for this," Death said when we lay together in the hospital, the dying all around us. Death was excited. Ready. She'd been long napping, and the stretch awake felt good to Her. From this moment forward, whether I lived to be 100 or 51, She was no longer a silent passenger. She would be my closest companion. Maybe the tears are for that awakening—the hospital's claws ripping open my belly compartment where Death sleeps next to the same place where Life begins.

Wake up, Death.

Wake up, Laraine.

It's time.

Maybe the tears are for the awareness that—for real—I would not escape not dying. I need to find a way to live while holding that truth in front of me, not stuffed in a "someday box." I need to bring Death *into* my story, not hold Her at arm's length until the ending.

Dear Death, how can we work together?

My tears are also angry ones. I, in fact, wouldn't escape Her. How the seduction of magical thinking had convinced me I was the one who would. And then the underneath that is always the underneath: Dad.

Where did you go? When Death came for you, was She already your friend? Or did you fight with Her like you did when you were seven in the polio ward surrounded by paralyzed, dying children? When you went with Her, was it sweet and gentle? Did She bring you a pair of working legs? A strong heart? A child's gaze? Did She bring you who you were before the world marked you? And if She did that, did you recognize your face?

Buddycat was warm and purring the morning he died, his chin resting in my palm. He purred even when he closed his eyes for the last time. We buried him in the backyard because no matter how long I've lived in the West, I am Southern and I want my dead surrounding me. I want to plant flowers over them and watch the butterflies and dragonflies come. My husband and I talk about death now. He wants to be cremated. I want to be wrapped in the roots of a new tree and planted. It sounds perfect. In theory. In the far-away abstraction. But my abstraction now has form. My abstraction is beginning to have color. Texture. Her eyes are green like mine.

I have become obsessed with an old Snoopy cartoon. Snoopy and Charlie Brown are sitting on a pier looking out over the water. "Someday, we will all die, Snoopy!" says Charlie Brown. "True," says Snoopy. "But on all the other days, we will not." My story lies in all the other days. The hospital, my diagnostic codes, my survival statistics will not write my story.

"Can't you tell me, Dad?" I cry to the empty bedroom. "What is it like? Where are you?"

I miss you.

I don't remember you.

I remember photographs of you. Stills etched in my mind, rewritten as memories.

I would walk past you if I saw you. There was once a time when I saw you in every man I saw on the street.

I don't remember you, but I always remember you.

When I hear one of the few recordings we have of your voice, it doesn't sound like the voice of yours that lives in my head. I try to make it so, but I can't. I remember it deeper, a baritone, not a tenor.

The words I remember you saying are the words I have in your letters that I have memorized. The ones that came on birthdays and Christmas, and occasionally on days when you noticed I was upset, or when you knew we were drifting apart and feared you would die before we could find our way back to each other.

You did, I guess.

And I've been trying to find my way back to you ever since.

I'm realizing that your Death isn't my Death. Not in form or timeline. Maybe your Death appeared to you as a golfer, or a history professor, or a hound dog. Maybe your Death gave you Her name back in 1949 when you lay in the polio ward and then reminded you of it when you lay in the ICU in 1976 and again in 1983. I hope your Death had soft arms, honeysuckle breath, and a Southern accent. Today I'm wondering if your Death opened back up Her arms to release you just a little bit—just enough of you to visit me when Buddycat's Death held open the door. Are our Deaths friends? Did they exchange time-tables and landscapes? Did they compare notes and walk parallel paths?

The sun is setting. My cat is dead. You are dead, and I have outrun my Death, for now.

Raven

I see I see I see from sea to shining sea and I know that when you write these things you are offering an incantation a prayer a spell that holds me well with no expectation that I change no promulgation that I leave you to your restless peace on seas so choppy you can't float can't breathe can't rest, oh daughter, look at me my beak my wings my feet look at me and see that I am ruined.

Me

You stand there, left leg longer than the other, one wing larger than the other, a perfect corvid representation of your human form. I don't see you ruined. I see you perfect, but I know that what I remember about you is viewed through distorted glasses, an expired prescription lens.

Raven

You remember me in frozen particles as ice crystals in your snow globe and you keep revisiting the places where we cracked while believing familiarity with the destination keeps you safe but you're not safe and I'm not safe and it's only folly all of these attempts to use your will to hold life still I may have died but I kept moving even underground I moved as flesh became food became another organism entirely does it surprise you, daughter, that I watch my own body dissolve look, daughter, look at thirty years my teeth are still in place on sheets of silk but my attacked heart is no longer to be found.

Me

In the months after you died, I saw you everywhere. In crosswalks. Alone on barstools in dim restaurants, a single whiskey sour in your hand. In passenger seats of American cars with white vinyl interiors. You waved to me and I waved back, but before I could say anything you vanished into the crowd or you slipped to the restroom or you sped up at the light. What astonishes me most to be talking to you now is that you didn't stay the same. You kept changing even after death, but I have spent thirty years holding onto a fixed form while you have kept becoming without me. Without Mom.

I'm afraid that I would pass you on the street today. I wouldn't recognize who you would be—a man nearing eighty. Would you have any hair left? You had precious little of it in your forties. Would you be able to walk at all, or would the polio that was returning in the months before your death have claimed your legs? Beneath your folded lids, would your eyes still be clear blue or would cataracts have hazed them?

I thought you were waiting too.

I thought a family was a commitment.

Raven

Daughter, I can tell you one thing now that I could not tell you before what they do not tell you about illness is that it is a ghost.

Once an illness bites you it leaves its saliva in your blood and you spend your days in one of two uncomfortable places—pretending that you're not haunted by its simmer in your cells or yelling at it from a broken limb of rage demanding it exorcise itself but it cannot because it is part of you mixing blending seeping into all that you are and you can no more remove yourself from illness than illness can remove itself from you and there comes a time when you must choose.

Me

Choose what?

Raven

Choose how you will live with the ghosts that chose you.

Me

I chose you. You're my ghost.

Raven

No, daughter, no I am not what you have made of me I am my own broken wing my own infected thing my own haunted haunting. To you I am who you have wished for but you should know your wish and my expression contain repressions deeper than the two of us can go.

Me

Is there no part of you that's you?

Raven

The part of me that's me is you.

Me

I have to stop again. Please. Wait.

Raven

_____.

Me

My thoughts exceed the pace of breath. I need a minute. But what is a minute in this time outside of time? My life has doors with names now: Survival statistics. Recurrence odds. Genetic probability. Six-month windows between scans in which I must live all the lives in case one of the doors decides to close for good. Each six-month span a held inhale; the exhale coming when the doctor calls and says, "Okay for now, okay," and then the inhale-hold until the next scan until the next call that says...

I can't count on what the next call says. I need to change the perception of time.

Raven

You need to learn how to live with a ghost.

Me

I have always lived with a ghost.

Raven

No. You have always lived with a wish do not mistake a yearning for a ghost. Illness breaks you into fractions makes you face your own subtraction but I can also tell you that diminishment and replenishment are sisters.

Me

I get it! Cancer is a ghost. Your heart attacks were ghosts. Your polio was a ghost.

Raven

No no no you obfuscate you iterate you think too literally for someone so attached to metaphors the doors are not the way inside the windows only reflect the pictures of your mind the truth is right inside your sentence look beneath the words and find your roots.

We all have those two lives, daughter, the second one begins the moment you realize the first one will end and so the ghost you host once you have met the face of illness is your own and no amount of chanting changing begging pleading can remove it because it is your own second life and it is up to you to make a friend of it a true companion a forever home inside your bones because once it has awakened it is most invested in your recognition of its needs.

Illness is a commitment.

Me

Wellness is too.

Raven

Yes but wellness will not take away the specter of your second life it will not make it so you will not see your own transition will not make it so your shadow walks behind you. Wellness makes your shadow longer stronger if you strive for balance because the healthier you are the louder death must be to keep up with your living it is half of the equation not an afterthought a thought to ponder after you have done all the things you hope to do. Take the hand of your second life, daughter, that is what I could not do I see I see from sea to sea but I did not see when I was living and I tried to beat it down my second life and you know, daughter, don't you I had three lives not two my shadows outnumbered my light my fright absorbed my life.

Me

Three lives?

Raven

Polio took my first life started my second life and then my attacked heart started the third but I had not understood that there could be more than one life yet not until I find myself here with you with my shortened leg the same as when I walked my fiery heart the same as when I talked it's only now that I see that I had three and my job now is to turn those three to one to be done to be free.

Me

Where will you go?

Raven

_____.

Me

What good is this conversation if you can't tell me that?

Raven

Isn't the conversation enough? Isn't the prayer always if you could have one more chance to talk one more walk in the rain one more kiss one more touch then you wouldn't miss so much hurt so much need so much isn't that the prayer the wish the desperate call in the middle of the night?

Me

It is, but it also isn't. I don't want a conversation. I want everything.

I have always been greedy.

Raven

When I died there was no one waiting for me, so I stayed. I stayed and you opened your arms to me and held me close and so we grew together like that, me wrapped in your bones, and that felt right and safe. That felt like home until it didn't and I needed to grow but your bones had settled into a cage and you had stretched your skin so tight over mine that if I moved I would destroy you. I had no choice but to make you bleed so you would cut me out and I could fly.

Me

I didn't realize I had grown so lopsided. My flesh had absorbed your story. My cells merged with yours until they began to mutate, and the parts of you I could not release grew roots into my colon wall and made a tumor. My coping pattern (everything is fine everything is fine) extended even to my DNA, ensuring that the cancer stayed hidden in plain sight, its mutations encapsulated in a dome of normalcy. When I finally began to bleed, the last desperate attempt of my own body to wake me up, I still ignored it. The wound had become so familiar I didn't want to be without it.

Who would I be without you? Who would I be if I were no longer the person who couldn't let go?

❦

Raven's Father

Son, like your daughter, we told the doctors no. They wanted to cut your Achilles tendon. It was standard practice, but we all knew the doctors were stabbing in the dark with so much polio, so many children lying in iron, so many children whose young muscles had collapsed. I can't even remember why they thought that would be useful, but your mother and I, we had a knowing that was wrong. We took you north to Baltimore to Johns Hopkins to the best doctors in all the country and it took all our money, but it was you, son, you, and we had a knowing.

Your mother called it the voice of God, but God had already left me, so I don't know what I'd rightly call it, except for knowing. Those knowings save us, I think, whether we think they come from God or not. This one saved you. You were able to walk. You were able to play golf well enough to make the world take note for a while. Our miracle boy. I reckon if I could get to you, you'd tell me you had a knowing to move away from us, and maybe that gave you a little more time. I hope to one day ask you. But I've been thinking about this: knowings don't always line up with wantings. That feels important to ponder now that I'm walking wearing just my bones to find you. Now, my knowing and my wanting are the same and that makes me right suspicious, but I'm already out of the dirt and I don't know how to put myself back in, so I might as well keep going.

Raven

When I pushed out of the desert dirt on the day of my burial the blue blankness of the sky made me fall back into my grave. No one was waiting for me. The sun had baked my bones. There was no shade, no damp, no song of creek and sea.

Me

When I walked away from your grave, as close to the single tree as possible, I heard the rustling in the ground. Must be a rabbit in the bush. A lizard maybe or a desert dove. My rational mind found reasons that could be quantified and verified, but even so, the rustling was under the earth and I knew it would draw me back to you.

Raven's Father

Son, I never visited your grave. I never came in life to touch the stone, to rub wax paper and pencil across the epitaph—*He walked by faith*—to sit alone on the grass until the sun set and the desert night animals showed their eyes. If I had come in life, perhaps I would not have to go in death, but I am coming, son. I am coming to bring you home.

Raven

There is a difference in the soil.
There is a difference in the sky.
There is a difference in the birds, the bugs, the slugs.
The music it is different here.
The sentences, the paragraphs
the voices.

Where are the voices?

Raven's Father

Son?

Raven

Dad?

Me

Dad! It's me! Where are you?

Raven

Dad! It's me! Where are you? I've wandered so far from home.

Me

I've wandered so far from home.

Raven's Father

Son.

Raven

I had to pull myself up up up from earth and into air I could not rest I could not sleep. Death it is not sleep it is movement it is steep steep climbing into space new pace new grace it is shedding skin for feather it is blending past with future it is going going home.

I must go back to creek to polio bed to mother father childhood rage to sand to sea to sea to shriek in flight across the stage till curtain falls and all around dissolves to light.

I need my people.

Me

After your headstone was placed, I went to the cemetery to visit. I brought a pillow, a blanket, water, and a peanut butter and apple jelly sandwich. I brought a tape deck to play Kenny Rogers music for you, and my journal to read things to you. I went in the dark after the services were done and the regular visitors had gone. I parked on the street in case they locked the gates, and once I had spread my blanket over the still-new grass above your coffin, a clot of stuck air released from my chest and I felt at last I could breathe.

Resthaven Cemetery is a sole patch of green in the dusty desert of West Phoenix. We'd chosen a space for you that was as close to a hedge of oleander as possible, a small reminder of North Carolina, an unexpected splash of color in a beige and brown setting. Because the grounds were cared for, the earth smelled damp like I remembered from North Carolina, like it hardly ever smells in Phoenix.

Desert nights are cool, even if the day has been over 100 degrees, and that night was no different. Bells chimed every fifteen minutes from the sanctuary where services were held. The half-moon suited me. I felt half-alive, but when I lay down on the earth, my belly to your belly, I was whole.

Raven

The dead are always watching. I should have found a way not to watch. A way to look away.

Me

Who am I talking to?

Raven

Hope.

❧

Raven's Mother

I remember that morning. The one when you stopped walking. So hot we like to have melted in our beds, but you froze instead. Your covers a mix of fire and ice; your skin bright red and shivering.

It was Tuesday. I thought we would be doing our usual summer things. You were going to help your daddy out in the field for a spell and your sister and I were going visiting with plates of our tomatoes and okra. I had made sunny-side-up eggs for your breakfast and I'd already set the grits to steaming in butter and salt.

Raven's Father

I came in from the field and hung up my hat. I went to knock on your door because you hadn't come out yet and when I reached your room I knew. I don't remember if you were screaming or silent, but I knew. Wilbur was thumping his tail on the braided rug and pawing at the door. "Mother," I called out, and she came and said—

Raven's Mother

"Fool, what are you standing outside the door for? Boy's got to get up." Your daddy just stood there like a scarecrow, his hand hovering over the doorknob like he seen a spook. Later he told me he felt it, and that made me feel even more lonely for you. I was your mother and I should have known.

Raven's Father

You were lying in sweaty sheets.

Raven's Mother

Your face was red.

Raven's Father

Your eyes were open.

Raven's Mother

Your throat was closed. "Go get the car," I said to your daddy. "Go get the car." And he did, and that was the last time he and I were truly husband and wife, though we lived together sixty more years. He went to you and I went away from you because I couldn't hold your suffering.

Raven's Father

I got the Buick and pulled it to the front of the house. Your mother carried you out and put you in the back seat. "We've lost him," she said, but I said, "No. We will never lose him. I will follow him for all my days."

Raven's Mother

I told him he was a fool again. Told him we had your sister to think of. Ourselves. We needed to pray. It was what I knew to do, son. When I reached for his hand on the ride to the hospital he stared straight ahead. He'd left me for you, and one day you'd leave me for your wife, and I did as I knew I would do. I was the last one standing. I buried you all.

Raven's Mother

I'd been growing more forgetful, it's true, and I left the stove on once when I wasn't cooking anything, and I forgot to write down where I left my car when I went to the A&P, but those things ain't enough to take a woman from her home. I've been speculating that it's not that I'm forgetting, it's that I'm remembering differently, and because I'm remembering differently, I'm doing things that seem odd. That don't mean nothing is wrong. Just means the things I see in front of my eyes aren't what they used to be.

But I know it ain't really any of that. It's because I talk to you, and to your daddy, and that makes her uncomfortable. Makes her think something's wrong with me, but, son, I never felt more right in my life. Nothin's more right than saying all the things you didn't ever get to say, even if you say them to a ghosted house.

For a moment, lying in my bed that last morning—still on my side of the bed even though your father has been gone for six years—I thought I could step back into the kitchen where we'd played canasta and everybody who used to be there would be there again. I didn't have to try hard to make myself hear the cards shuffling, the ice clinking in the sweet tea glasses.

Son, I was born with the egg that made you. I was born carrying your life, and when you left, my belly went numb and it never did get any feeling back.

I have to go to the bathroom. There. I finally heard you. *Mama.* There, son. Mama's coming.

I put my feet on those hardwood floors right in the dust of your own footsteps. The wood remembers. Right over there, by the bathroom door, is where you fell after we brought you back from the hospital and they told you you wouldn't walk again. Your daddy wouldn't believe it and I thought it was best we listen to the doctors so we could move forward, but you had rolled yourself out of the bed and pulled yourself up by climbing the wall with your tiny fingers and then you fell, but you didn't make a sound. You lay there a minute and then started to pull yourself up again. I wanted to go help you but your daddy held me back. "Look at his eyes," he said—and I did—and yours were focused on something so precise—so far away—that I knew some part of you was two thousand miles from this house. I didn't know an eight-year-old could have so much anger.

Mama. I hear you, son. I'm coming. Just let me get to the bathroom. Let me make a pot of coffee. Sit on the porch. Watch the creek. Sun's up now, over the water, and all the drops of dew are shining like tears of joy. I never quite saw it like that before. All these years living here, you'd think I'd have seen it in all the ways.

The coffee is bitter. I left it on the stove too long. Burned it a touch. Feeling some grounds ticking between my teeth. Won't be long now. Your sister's car with its fancy tires will pull up behind me—that crunch on the gravel a signal to move on down the road. Sitting here, picking at the grounds in my teeth, I know I'll never hear them tires coming. I'll already be gone.

I have been thinking a lot about death since everyone up and died. I knew your daddy would go before me. He was never as strong—though I hear what y'all say—never as mean as me, but I'm not mean I'm determined. They're not the same. I'm afraid of it, not going to lie, but either Jesus is waiting for me or He ain't and it's too late to change that answer.

The white cat came by that morning. I'd been feeding her a year or so, letting her rub around my feet, scratch a bit at the door. Never let her in of course. Cats are for outside, but she's been good company. Who'll look after her once they take me to the home? Your sister will never do it. Neighbors won't. I tell her, "Cat, you got to figure it out on your own now. I've got to go." She didn't say anything back. Don't you get thinking the cat always talks back to me. She doesn't. Not always.

I give her some extra chicken from the bone and I was working myself up to a proper goodbye but she turned and ran off into the woods after a squirrel or some such. That's how it is though, ain't it? Never time for the goodbye like you read about. Just one day something is there and the next minute it ain't.

Was the cat made me think I could do it. Be here and then gone. I pressed my palm on that old screen door. The one that always stuck and then would slam shut. Your daddy made the door, like he made the whole of the house, and I could see the land before it was ours, and then board by board, nail by nail, he made a house. Made a pier that you jumped from. Made a garden.

I didn't know how to say goodbye to the house. It wasn't going to disappear on me like the cat, but I was disappearing on it and that felt rude and disrespecting, considering all it's done for us. All it's put up with being alone with just me.

So I moved into the house from the side porch, like I done every day for sixty years, and I triple checked the stove was off, the icebox closed, the fans turned still. I went to the living room and sat on the high-backed sofa in front of the fireplace that your daddy got up to light every morning in winter and I could see him there, stooped, feeding the wood to it, adjusting the flue. I could see him so much I thought I could touch him, reached my hand out even, but you caught it.

Mama. Mama. Wake up.

My black pocketbook rested on my lap. Inside, your sister will find peppermints, salt and pepper I took from the buffet line, my wallet, a package of Kleenex, and my red lipstick. My legs were crossed at the ankles as I'd always been taught. The fireplace was empty. The cat was gone. My spine was straight. Your sister was a mile out in her fancy car with the fancy tires. She'd be pulling into the driveway in less than five minutes. I would still be warm.

It turns out all it takes to leave is to let go.

I was still sitting upright when I became something new. I reached for the white curl of my hair, wanted to blot at the corners of my lips, but I could only reach, not touch. I was both in my house and out of my house and it was the most natural

191

thing it could be. Your sister had pulled into the driveway. She sat in the car a moment before coming in to get me. I regretted not leaving her a note, but it was too late. My mouth had begun to open and for a minute I thought I might breathe again. Dead is a constant exhale.

Outside the house, the white cat slept in an old planter out behind our barn. Her ears flicked with her dreams. The house grew farther away, your sister walked closer to me, I stayed stretched between all of it. But when she opened the front door, I tumbled out of the room away from my body away from the fireplace away from our home. I didn't see her find me. I never saw her again.

I was trying to remember the words I was taught in church. Who was supposed to meet me? Where were the gates and the clouds and the saints? But the words started falling out of me so fast I couldn't catch them. All those verses. All those promises. Tumbling like a waterfall, dissolving into spray.

I wasn't given any chance to decide where to go—up or down, left or right. I was pulled into the dark and on the black wall the movie began. It was 8mm film, bouncing and bubbling, my whole life in faded color.

It wasn't the images that gripped my throat. I had pictures of you. Of your daddy and me. Of my parents.

It was the sounds.

I hadn't heard my father's voice in decades and to hear it scratched and vibrating from the wall stopped me. All around me the sounds began. Papa on one wall. Mother on the other. Your daddy. You. They circled me, chatting up the day, but not ever talking to me directly. I spun and spun trying to catch one of the voices, trying to look one of you in the eye, but it wasn't possible. This place held all of me and I couldn't touch one bit of it. I couldn't find where the movie was being projected from and I couldn't figure out where to go next. There were no doors, no windows. Just a movie on repeat. Just those moments where I had caused someone to hurt. But what about me I tried to scream but I had no voice. No voice in a room of voices. Is that how I made you feel, son?

I want to go back to the house, to my body, to my open mouth and stiffening fingers. Where am I? This is not what I thought it would be.

"Connell," he says, your daddy says, and the movie stops, the frame on the wall in front of me on our wedding day. "Before," he says. "Let's go before," and his hand extends from the wall, too long, too rubbery, but I take it because it's the first thing in this place that has reached for me. "Connell," he says. "We've got to find our boy."

21

The places I visit in Tucson—the Modern Languages Building, Antigone's, The Blue Willow, they aren't the right places. They aren't where the fracturing happened. By the time I wandered those areas, I'd already been cut. The parts of me I'm hoping to find never went there.

I don't remember the address of the apartment complex where D— and I lived, but my body remembers how to get there. Two blocks south of the Bashful Bandit biker bar sits The Royal El Con Apartments, four floors of small units arranged in a rectangle around a dirty swimming pool and grill. When I lived there, the doors were painted teal, the balcony railings a rusted dusty rose. In 1987, they were sketchy apartments, but the price was right. $250 for a 600-square-foot one-bedroom, utilities included. In 2019, there's no doubt of the drug trade in the parking lot, the meth kitchens behind the darkened windows, the squatters on mattresses in the parking lot where I'd long ago parked my old AMC Spirit, adding oil every three days to keep her running. The doors have been repainted to a hunter green, but the balcony railings remain the sick shade of pink, the rust all the more noticeable after thirty years of neglect.

I park my car in the front this time, next to a station wagon with three flat tires. I don't remember my apartment number, but my feet remember the number of steps from parking lot to door, and I arrive at A34. There is no doubt this is the right place. The wrong place.

I stand in front of the door, aware of dozens of pairs of eyes on me from other apartments. The windows watch here. Three people are inside my apartment. Through a slat in the blinds, I see one man lying on the floor of the living room. Two others are in the bedroom. There's no bed, just clothes on the floor and a giant television under the window. I can almost span the length of the apartment with my arms and for the first time I realize how small the apartment was. How close D— and I had to be to live there. It had seemed so big then. Maybe because I was so small. I can imagine the tiny kitchen, where D— made stuffed peppers and then threw a knife at me, lodging it in the wall beside my head. "If I'd wanted to hit you, I would have," he'd said. From what I can tell peering in through the gap in the blinds, it looks like the same carpet is there—a filthy beige. When I lived there, the tile in the bathroom had come up, revealing dirt and grime on a base cement floor. My orange cat, Apricot, had gotten lost between the apartments when she went into a hole in the tiny hall closet.

I'm worried the occupants know I'm there. It's dusk and soon the complex will come alive with the people who deal in darkness, and I'll be caught between the worlds once again. I imagine one of them has a gun pointed at my chest through the door, but I don't know if I'm conflating the time D— pointed a gun at me. Or the time, when he was sleeping, that I pointed that same gun at him and as I sat on the edge of our bed, the .38 heavy and foreign in my hands, I knew that I could kill him, and that if I decided to, I would not miss. I could see my life unfurling from that shot. Premeditation. Cold-blooded. Calculated. Arizona is a death penalty state. I did not want that ending to my story, but as I watched him sleep, mouth parted innocent as a child's, my heart calmed. I would not kill him. But I was capable of it, and there was a power to that. I was coming back to life. I put the gun back in its case, slid it under the bed, and knew I would get out. But it wouldn't be for a while.

I can still see the answering machine on the metal end table where my father had called me from death.

"Sugar, get out."

His voice reverberated within the walls. I hold my hand above the door, wanting to touch it, but afraid of who might walk out. If I touch it, will it suck me back in? If I don't touch it, will I be still circling, a shimmering fish unsure what happened to her life?

After D— moved out, I cleared away everything that was his. I bought a new single bed. New sheets. Another cat. The dishes that remained were mine. The shampoo. The hangars. The towels. He took his gun and I've never had a firearm in my house again. I hear voices inside the apartment. They aren't mine. They aren't D—'s. They aren't Dad's.

I was twenty when I lived here.

I walk to the rear staircase down to the parking lot. Rusted trucks rest on top of cinder blocks. Three used mattresses dot the cement. The dumpster lid is open and trash peeks out. Walking down the stairs is easy. Walking back up is the problem.

I go to my old covered parking space, which is now occupied by a tan VW bug with a cracked windshield. I worked at AMC El Con Cinemas when I lived here. I was a projectionist, working late evenings, studying in the darkened area above the theater seats. D— always thought I was cheating on him, and eventually I did, returning to the lover I had in Phoenix, my first love who was never the right love, but smelled of safety and Tide. A few months into the affair, I told him that if anything happened to me, he needed to point the police toward D—. I felt like a character in the most melodramatic of books. A broken, abused woman, cheating on her partner and preparing for her untimely death. I had so succeeded in reinventing myself that I no longer recognized the costume or the script I was in.

D— made up all sorts of nefarious scenarios about what he thought I was really doing when I was working and one night I came home particularly late. Our last movie of the night was three hours long and didn't start until 10:15 p.m. He was waiting for me beneath the slabbed stairs. The parking lot was ill lit. I was tired. I had an eight a.m. class. When I reached the third step, he reached between the stairs and grabbed my ankle, pulling me down, my chin banging on the cement, my teeth cleaving my tongue. I didn't know it was him at first. It was two in the morning. It could have been anyone. I tried to reach through the steps to grab him and kick my leg free, but he had leverage and he hadn't been surprised. When he spoke, I knew it was him, but that wasn't as comforting as you'd think. *This is how he kills me*, I thought. On the steps. In the dark. When I'm wearing polyester.

I don't remember what he screamed, only that he screamed and pulled me up and into the house where he ripped the sleeve of my white oxford work shirt as he clawed at me, pulling my pants down to shove his fingers inside, searching for someone else's semen. He stopped screaming, locked the door, and pushed me face down onto the bed, the blood from my chin staining the sheets his mother gave us. He kicked apart my legs, raising me up to my knees, and when he entered me I felt relief. It would be over soon. My tongue throbbed and when his belly slapped against my hips I came. He bit at the back of my neck, cupped each cheek, and then slid his fingers around my neck and pressed just enough. He kept thrusting and I let myself surrender to it. It would be easier, I knew, for him to believe I wanted it. It would be easier if he thought he'd won. It wouldn't be long now and when he released his grunt to the walls, he fell on top of me. "If you leave me, I will kill you," he said. "Clean yourself up." And he left the apartment and I curled into the stink of the sheets.

Apricot had watched from the corner, bent tail swishing. "I will get us out," I said to her, and I pulled up my pants and went to the bathroom to clean the scrapes on my face, the ones that I could tell a truth about when people asked at work. "Oh, I fell down the stairs." And they'd not push for more even though everyone knows almost no one falls down the stairs for no reason.

That story is a cliché. A familiar narrative that no one wants to read about anymore because it's not sensational. It's *common*. And it was supposed to happen to other people who made different choices than I did, except that's a myth too, and it happens to just about every woman I know to some degree and still—this is the first time, thirty years later, that I'm talking about it. Because it was *common*. Because it was boring. Because I came. Because I let him in. Because I played along. Because I had agreed to marry him. Because my father had died and I had nowhere else to go and I had made my choice and once I make a commitment *I do not let go.*

After D— moved out, I pushed my new single bed against the wall, leaving no place for anyone to sneak in. No one talked about consent in 1987. Rape was for alleys and alcohol and bars. Rape wasn't for bedrooms with people you knew. Rape wasn't for girls with a 4.0 GPA at college, who worked full time, who came from "good" families, who only occasionally fell down the stairs or fell asleep during class. I could have left him, I say to the hunter green door. To A34.

Sugar! Get out!

I could have called home. I could have asked for money. I could have moved away. I wasn't alone, but I had isolated myself. I had resources but I couldn't ask for them because then I'd have to figure out what role I was playing, what script I was cast in and more importantly, who had written the play.

So I stayed.

Abuse is a commitment.

I start up the stairs. One, two, three. Stop. This was the step. My body remembers the position of the railing to my shoulder, the number of steps left to climb (two) when he pulled me under. I go back to the parking lot and start again. One, two, three. Stop. Back to the parking lot. One, two, three, four. Thud. I grip the rail. My twenty-year-old self lies there in present tense, her ankle gripped from beneath, the ankle she will struggle with for decades. The ankle she will fall and twist, fall and twist, until it perpetually aches. I stay standing. She pants. Squeezes her eyes closed. *Daddy, where are you?*

D— is shouting again, his voice a worn groove in my heart. *You will never be anything. You do everything half-assed. You will never be a writer. You will never be anything. If you leave me, I will kill you.*

And I am sure he's right because I don't know how to leave people.

Or places.

Or diagnoses.

Twenty-year-old me is a paper doll, flat and fragile. For decades people have walked over her on these steps. They don't see her. They don't hear her. She took her rage and swallowed. She is fine, she is fine, she is fine. She doesn't need any help. She can do it all herself. She made the funeral calls. She gave the eulogy. She wrote the epitaph. She's the only one who remembers everything. Everything. She promised Daddy she would not forget him, would not let his story go, would not be alive without him and her cells heard her words and got to work holding, holding, holding.

My heart leaps to its stress arrhythmia. The sun will sink in twenty minutes. I pick up the other foot and set it down. Thud. I was a size 2 then. Now I am a size 12. I have room for her in the folds of my scarred belly, underneath the sway of my breasts. She waits for his rage so she can swallow it and make it hers, lap at it with the tip of her bruised tongue, cool his unpredictability with her damp. A car backfires on Grant Street. I crouch, one hand still grasping the rail, the other reaching for twenty-year-old me's hair. I stroke it. It was long and thick then, and he liked to pull it like horse's reins when he rode her, liked to slap her flank when she came.

"He's gone," I whisper but she doesn't move, she's been so long trampled on these steps. "Come on." When she pushes herself up, the steps have held her impression. Ten more minutes until dark. "We have to go." She puts her hand in mine, a silver ring on each finger, her armor. I straighten her maroon work vest, the polyester clip-on bow tie. I climb the final steps, my arm tight around her waist. When we reach the landing, she doesn't want to go any farther. Doesn't want to go to A34, but we have to so she can see she's not there anymore. It's seventeen steps from the landing to the apartment door. I wait for her while she slips inside, touching the scar on the wall from the knife, standing in the bedroom where Apricot watches, yellow eyes glowing. She slides back under the door, her cat in her paper-doll arm. I press my thumb against the cut on her chin. "You didn't fall down the stairs. You were pushed. And you lived." She dives into my belly, between the five robot-kiss scars, Apricot's tail the last glint of orange I see as my belly button closes.

It's night now, and I am full.

Raven

A father is supposed to protect.
Caw-caw-caw-caw!
Daughter daughter.
I tried.

Raven's Father

A father is supposed to protect.

I let polio in the house. I don't know how I did that, but it was my job to keep you safe and so there must have been some window I did not close, some door I did not lock. Your mother blamed me and so I grew quieter than I was before until I was nothing but a bent shadow in the room. I'm grateful that you never had to see your daughter sick. Helpless is not a strong enough word.

The doctors wouldn't let us see you. No one knew exactly how polio spread and we had your sister to think about, but at night I'd lie awake on the hot sheets and imagine myself with you in your frozen bed and try to will your dead leg to come to mine instead. Night after night this was my prayer. Lord, pass this on to me. I thought a lot about God then and how he let his son be killed and I started to crack a little. There was no way he was a father. A father would have climbed on that cross instead.

I kept these thoughts to myself, like I kept all my thoughts to myself, and I grew thinner and thinner until even I would stand in front of a mirror and see right through my bones. I tried to recall when I had lost my form—the form of father—but the moment of moving from visible to invisible was untraceable. I stood outside your hospital ward's doors, staring at the word *quarantine*, trying to make sense of why you were on one side of a door and I was on the other. I felt like that when you died too. I was on one side and you were on the other and then I was try-ing to remember the last time I heard your voice, the last words we said, but they had vanished like my form. I lived for twelve seasons after you, but if you asked me what I did then, what I thought, where I went, I could only tell you "backwards." I went backwards. I thought backwards. Every day was wrapped in past and your mother and I grew farther and farther apart until she was also on one side of a door and I the other.

I think the last thing I said to you was, "We're certainly looking forward to seeing you in October." You had called to tell us you'd bought tickets for the Homecoming at the church and long distance calls were expensive so conversations were short. Did you hear what was underneath each of those words? I can tell you now.

There is not a day that goes by that you don't cross my mind.

When I see you, you are not the boy with polio, the boy who had a heart attack, the boy who could not work. You are only my boy, and I will always remember you running with Wilbur through the yard. Do you remember? One foot and then the other—strong, sure, stable.

I count the days to your visits, to when we can walk the fields, go to the golf course, sit on the porch and say nothing.

Did you hear all that underneath my words? This is what I want you to feel now, son: my breath beneath the sounds. Can it carry you back to us?

❧

Raven's Father

Your mother made a funeral for you that would have rivaled a saint's, but she never used the word *dead* to talk about you. You were always just about to walk in the door, just about to tell a joke, just about to do something to make her mad. She held to those "just about to-s" until the end. I sat next to her on our high-backed sofa in the parlor in front of the fireplace where we helped you practice your steps, both of us in sweltering black, playing the parts. I say playing, son, not because we didn't grieve, but because it simply had to be playing. If we weren't acting, then there was no reason to start another day.

When I died, I knew I had one more chance to find you. So here I am. I know you're waiting for me too.

∽

Me

When I returned from Tucson, Mom had gotten married again.

Raven

_____.

Me

When I went to Tucson, you had just died. I was only gone two years. She kept moving.

Raven

You did not see what I saw did not see what she had gone through did not see the ways she moved inside our house without me. I watched and perched and held the walls of the house with my wings while she gave away things and rearranged her cells so that she could move into her second life my wife my wife but my wings never let go my wings never stopped wrapping her tight but she couldn't stay with me and live right. Remember when we took a drive and I told you she would find another person and that I had told her that was fine and you looked out the window not at me and I knew it wasn't fine for you but maybe now that you're in second life maybe now that you're past middle age you see something you could not see back then that she could love me and also him that she could laugh and be alive and that it didn't mean anything about her and me that love was bigger do you see, my daughter, do you see?

Me

I felt like she had become someone else. I was still your daughter but she was not your wife.

Raven

My life my wife my wife. A family is a commitment.

Me

She has been married to him longer than she was married to you.

Raven

My wife my wife my wife. Daughter, you will see what I can see that certificates and documents are meaningful only on the earth and that relationships exist outside of them. Do not bookmark things with date stamps they tell you nothing of what's between them.

Me

When I went back to Phoenix after leaving D——, no one was where I left them. Mom was not a widow but a wife and I was still a daughter without you.

Raven

Caw caw caw I saw you standing at the wedding with her and him and I was there too at the edges in the blur and when she left with him and went to her new nest I stretched wide and let her go but you took me with you carried me from house to house and as each person you knew moved farther from me you grew angrier because you held tighter but see now don't you see that there is no leaving is no going is no staying only is. There only is the space between and in that place there is no wife no daughter no husband no father only family.

Me

Still, I see her hold his hand and I can't breathe.

21

My mother and I return to her childhood apartment in Bay Ridge, Brooklyn, in 2015. It had been fifty-two years since she moved away. She will tell you she is fine (always fine). She will tell you she doesn't miss New York. She will tell you that she has survived because she adapts, and that the past belongs in the past, no matter that I keep telling her the past wraps the present with its ribbons.

When we get to New York, she tells everyone—from the Uber driver to the waiter to the docent at the Brooklyn Museum—that she used to live here. "I lived in Bay Ridge," she says, and the young people smile at her and ask her about it.

We go to an Italian restaurant just a few blocks from her childhood apartment and when she tells the waiter she used to live here, the owner, a jolly man with a thick mustache and red-flecked eyes comes and sits at our table. "Right down the block," she says to him.

"It's sure changed," he says, his accent Sicily-thick, "but it's still our block."

He brings us grappa and a tiramisù to split on the house, the lines as deep in his face as my mother's. "Welcome home, Bella," he says and raises a glass. My mother's green eyes water. There are framed color pictures of men, mostly emergency workers, who died on 9/11, arced across the foyer. Votive candles burn beneath them. They used to be here. They are here.

She wants to find a T-shirt that says Brooklyn. Even better, one that says Brooklyn Dodgers, a team that doesn't exist anymore, except that they do in that neighborhood, and they do in the mind of my mother, and it isn't actually hard to find a T-shirt that says Brooklyn Dodgers, and she makes me buy one for myself even though I don't wear T-shirts.

We walk toward her old apartment, which is a third-floor

walkup in a part of Brooklyn that used to be the end of the world but is now hip and full of babies and dogs in coats and juice bars. She stops a teenager on a bike wearing a shirt advertising a butcher. She points at the logo. "Do you work there?" I offer a reassuring nod to the boy who stops pedaling and talks to her.

"Yeah," he says. "I got a delivery to make."

"We used to get all our meat there," she says. "Is it still where it used to be?"

The boy shrugs. "I don't know where it used to be. I know where it is." He gives us directions and we go to visit the butcher, which is both where it used to be and where it is, a comfort to my mother and a comfort to me.

When we get to her apartment we stand in front of the old wood and glass doors. "We used to clean the stairs inside," she says. "The snow would come and make icy mud."

I stayed in that apartment once, on the only trip we made to visit her mother. She was an alcoholic, but she was also beautiful, and she won the Publisher's Clearinghouse Sweepstakes before she met my grandfather, and she could see the ghosts from Finland in the house. When we left her after that trip, she watched us drive away from the window, waving. I never saw her again, though she lived two more decades. I've frozen her there, waving at us, before she went back to get another drink.

My mother remembers her mother passed out. Angry. Demanding. *Haunted.* My mother did what she had to do. Graduated early. Moved away. Started over. When I tell her I see things sometimes, hear things sometimes, find stories in walls, she says, "My mother did that." To survive, my mother became a mathematician, building a life of logic and probability, a life of parallel lines. My lines are always intersecting.

"I want to go to the Brooklyn Zoo," she says, and so we catch another train. These trains are labeled with different letters than the ones she remembers. The IRT and the BMT lines are gone. The codes she knew that carried her home have been overwritten with new numbers. This frustrates her, and she tells me at every stop what the number used to be. Where the train used to go. Where she got off to go to work. Where she went to school. Where she went on the weekends to get away from the house.

The Brooklyn Zoo is now the Prospect Park Zoo, and it is small and we spend most of the time watching the sea lions and the cats. She's quiet. The zoo is where it always was but it is not what it used to be. We get a hot dog and a Diet Coke and sit on the plastic picnic tables and watch the children. We are in two different zoos.

On the way out, we stop at the carousel, which is exactly where it used to be and is exactly what it used to be, and when she used to ride it as a girl, it was already forty years old. The kid scrolling through his phone looks up when we get close. "There was always a line here," she says, and I can feel the swarm of children dancing in the light. No one is waiting today.

She opens her wallet to buy two tickets. "It used to be a nickel," she says and smiles. "Does it play the same song?" she asks the kid.

He shrugs. "I dunno."

We are the only two on the carousel. She walks between the horses, touching their painted manes, their glass eyes, the poles that impale their hearts. She finds the one she's looking for, a white stallion with a red saddle and fire-green eyes. Her horse is on the outer ring. I choose a horse beside her, inside toward the center. The kid starts the ride and the notes from the song are brassy. My mother stands up in the stirrups and holds the pole. She stretches out her right arm and waves at the kid as the carousel circles. She smiles wide as the rivers that the bridges span.

Her parallel lines have intersected.

"It's the same song," she says, and reaches for my hand. "It's the same song."

❧

Against all my doctors' advice, I travel again to New York City with my mother two months after my surgery in 2017. She talks

207

a lot in New York. At home in Arizona, she lets other people talk. I recognize this because I do the same thing. Other people will always talk about themselves if you let them, and we can stay hidden behind our smiles, our green eyes. Other people think they know us, but they don't because we never talk. We're all right with that, holding our selves close.

Our trip had been booked for almost nine months and most of it was non-refundable. If I could walk, I was going, and so I did.

Travel is a commitment.

I should not have gone. I'm not sleeping because my intestines haven't yet recalibrated and I have to go to the bathroom every thirty minutes or so, and each trip to the toilet takes about twenty minutes. *Most people's bowels find a new normal within a year,* the surgeon said. *Be patient. It won't be what it used to be.* New York is hard if you need bathrooms. New York is also hard if you don't have stamina. If you can't go blocks without stopping. If you can't keep pace with the crowd. I should not have gone, but if I had it to do over again, I would still go because going is not surrendering my story to the doctors' version. Going is rewriting the script. Going is establishing that my will is once again in charge.

When my mother lived in New York, the major museums were free on the weekends and so she spent her days away from her apartment, her mother, in the arms of art—sculpture, painting, archeology. Her love of museums has lasted a lifetime, and as anyone who's ever gone to a museum of any size with her can attest, the trip is a test of endurance. We call her a "plaque reader." She reads literally every caption, listens to every added commentary, enjoys all the short film features. Every. Single. One. Her favorite museum is the American Museum of Natural History, so we plan a day to spend there, followed by dinner with friends from my childhood. I'd never been before and I did not anticipate how many plaques.

There are plenty of exhibits at the museum that weren't there sixty years ago when she was a child standing in the Theodore

Roosevelt Rotunda in front of the dioramas, but she's not interested in those. She wants to go where she's been. Where what used to be still is.

The fourth floor holds the fossils. You can wander through Vertebrate Origins, Primitive Mammals, Ornithischian Dinosaurs, Saurischian Dinosaurs, the Wallace Wing of Mammals and Their Extinct Relatives, and the Milstein Hall of Advanced Mammals. The floor is crowded. Everyone loves dinosaurs. Dozens of languages fill the rooms and people take selfies with the bones of saber-toothed cats and giant tortoises. My mother reads the plaques. When we've spent two hours in only one room, I realize the challenge of the day. No one can read every plaque in this museum in one afternoon. We are going to have to choose what to see. We will not finish what we start.

Not in this museum. Not in this life.

I skip epochs ahead and take pictures of her getting in close to read about a fossil. I watch her at the interactive exhibits, lighting up when the machine gives her new information. I text the pictures to my husband and our friends we're meeting for dinner, wine glass emojis framing the photos. I'm tired. I can't stand very long and although I enjoy museums, I'm content with the highlight reels. My mother, though, continues to *learn*. She's seventy-six. "Isn't this fascinating?" she says and then returns to a plaque. "The world is amazing."

I need to sit, so I move to the dark Wallach Orientation Center, which is now home to the 122-foot-long cast of a Titanosaur. The skeleton is so long it can't be contained by the exhibit hall, and its head peers out at the entrance, barely clearing the high door frame. There are plenty of benches to sit on and gawk at its size. This dinosaur was recently discovered and wasn't part of the museum when my mother was a girl. She finds me in a corner and asks if I'm all right. "I'm fine," I say. She's learned something new and tells me and returns to the next fossil display.

This gigantic creature, this Titanosaur, took up so much space, died and settled into the earth, unremembered for millennia. Now, thousands of people look at its bones every week. It is not what it was when it lived, but it still exists. My father is not who he was when he lived, but he still exists. After he died, my mother remained: solid bones, wide smile, open heart. I watch her in black travel pants and a T-shirt, permed, thinning hair, sensible walking shoes, taking in the totality of life on earth, organized by periods of time. All her weekend visits to this museum taught her that form shifts but life continues.

This is how she could remarry, my father in her heart, her new husband in her heart. She stretched while I solidified.

My friend texts back: *How many bottles of wine should I have? ;-)*

I remember a line from a letter my father wrote to me on my eleventh birthday, three years after his heart attack:

When I was in the hospital, you wrote and told me that you would keep my watch wound so time would not run out. I cried when I read that, and I still do, because time runs out, as we think of it, but the ideas, the shared love, and the caring for others guarantee us to be immortal. Time shrinks, but love expands.

My mother sits next to me in front of this old-new dinosaur. Her eyes shine with wonder. "How do they keep finding bones?" I don't know. I'm a writer, not a paleontologist. I look at this skeleton cast and see a story, two-floors tall and 122 feet wide. I look at her and I see her story—at least three lives, each one packed in her cells, each one informing who she is. Who she is making me.

She notices my phone's screen. "You're making fun of me," she says and laughs.

"Yes," I say. "You're reading every plaque over the course of planetary history."

She moves closer to the skeleton. "I might not ever be back here."

Mom turns to me, her back toward the skeleton, framing her five-foot-two frame, which once was five foot four.

She used to be.

She is.

As many as you have, I text back. Wine emoji. Heart emoji. And then an extra heart emoji. Wine used to be grapes.

I stand and join her. And though we will never be back here again, we used to be, and so we are.

Raven

I see I see from sea to sea—

Me

Stop, Raven. I cannot talk to you now. Let me talk to the living.

Raven

_____.

22

The crack in the glass has reappeared, and Shadow-you is still making lists at her desk:
- take supplements
- schedule colonoscopy
- take Barnessa to the vet
- look at medical records again

She is thinner and fuller and you wonder how this can be, how she has also gone on without you. You're going to have to choose, or the choice will be made for you. Do you choose your second life or do you choose to stay with your father in the velvet dark?

Shadow-you hasn't quite stopped Googling survival statistics. She hasn't quite stopped believing every new bump or odd ache is recurrence. She keeps re-reading previous scans, making sure they say what she remembered. She is waiting for the words to rearrange themselves and surprise her, like the original diagnosis did.

The glass crack is not yet a door.

Shadow-you is drinking elderberry syrup each morning made from the honey of bees raised on the land her father grew up on. Her cousin lives there now, and his wife keeps bees and makes syrup and she sent her pints of sweet home nectar. For immunity. For family. From the land that's in your bones, even if it isn't yours.

You see she hasn't quite accepted that cancer doesn't have to be a part of every thought. She holds things. She is loyal, even to that which kills her.

Barnessa lives inside her house now, sleeping beside her head, one paw touching her all night. She is safe. *Until she is not.* That voice. That truth. She feels it. She cannot prevent the time when Barnessa will die.

She cannot prevent the time when she will die.

Shadow-you needs you or she will obsess and she will miss the time between now and when she will go. The Raven is agitated and you turn to help and see your grandmother and grandfather swirling around him, straw hat, string of pearls, a boy with a limp leg and a broken heart.

"We have walked so far," says grandfather.

"We didn't think we'd find you," says grandmother.

"I waited for you," says Raven. "I waited by my grave but then I had to go."

"She brought us here," says grandmother, and you're surprised she sees you. "She couldn't let us go without you."

"She's been trying to write us home for years," says grandfather.

"My leg," says Raven.

"Is perfect," says grandfather.

"Is part of us," says grandmother.

You are running out of time. Raven is farther away, his voice no longer pointed at you. His wings have raised and lifted straw hat, lifted pearls, and he is moving without you writing any lines.

"Daddy! This is my script! Our script! You can't go unless I write it!"

Raven looks at you with slanted sparking eye. "So, what will you do? Daughter, time is out."

Shadow-you is holding the wild cat, stroking her brick nose, and wondering how to love what will leave, wondering how to leave what she loves. The cat sleeps.

"You fed her," says Raven. "What you feed will stay."

"You never told me," you say.

"What?"

"What they don't tell you about illness."

"One more cigarette," he says. "Come closer."

Shadow-you is looking at her latest scan results again. Is there something she missed? Something she should pay attention to? She has at least a dozen files open on her computer. A pile of sticky notes rests near her hand.

You and Raven are within touching distance. The smoke burns your eyes but you're afraid to blink.

"They don't tell you illness remakes you into someone else. They want you to be who you were. Doctors. Family. Friends. But you will never be who you were. Don't spend whatever time you have left trying to return to before. That's a life lived backwards." He grinds his final cigarette to ash. "Which way are you going?"

The keyhole crack widens, and you pick up the feathered quill before the choice is made for you.

Raven

I see I see.

Raven's Father

From sea.

Raven's Mother

To sea.

Raven's Father

My son.

Raven's Mother

My son.

Raven

Daughter, I must.

Raven's Father

Son.

Raven's Mother

Son.

Raven

Sun I see I see the sun, daughter, do you do you see?

Me

I cannot see I cannot.

Raven

You can you can you see from sea to sea you see that you and me are moving—now I on tree and you and you and you remain on ground my sound within your throat my voice inside your heart, my daughter, we are not apart but we are separate separate separate separate we must be you and me must be from sea to sea you see I see you must know must know, daughter, I must go must go. Must. Go.

Me

_____.

Raven's Father

Son, it's me. Your feathers led me here and I admit that I thought I would wander ever farther from my grave until time extinguished into stars. But here you are. So beautiful. So perfect. My son. Come home. We will make you a place to rest.

Raven's Mother

You can never leave family. I've come for you like I promised you I would. From the day you were born, the day you pushed out of my own flesh I knew I would never leave you behind. I listened to you talk about me, watched you pull yourself away from me, but always I was there. I followed your footsteps, one solid and one slippery, and I know you from your heart.

Raven's Father

Wife.

Raven's Mother

Husband.

Me

I can't. Where will I go? What will I write? Who will I be?

Raven

Give me the quill this play has ended on this day your pen will write a different book where you will find without my shadow you can speak. Look, daughter, look, I am far away you cannot stay but I will watch will perch will wait and one day meet you greet you here again say it now unpack your throat put down this script don't hesitate there's only so much time you will have breath to walk on feet on broken shifting earth.

Your belly's scars have faded to the softest of brush strokes on skin. You lean against the double-paned glass, your back to your house, and watch what you had never thought you'd see on this sea or the other. In Raven's beak, a tube of tumored colon. In your hand, the quill made from his silky wing feather. The glass begins to crack. Shadow-you has been busy. She is full and pink and her eyes are lined with kohl. You touch her shoulder, which has grown more sturdy while you have been away.

Your grandfather, a wide-brimmed hat atop a wisp of blue-gray smoke, extends his fog around Raven's shortened leg. Your grandmother, a string of pearls around a veiny neck of white, strokes Raven's back with thick-ridged nails. They build a nest from twigs and soil they each had carried from their graves. Raven drops your tumored colon in the mix and pecks it apart until only fragments remain, glistening on the walls like jewels. His beak is open; his eyes flick one more shimmer at you before he sinks under hat beneath hand into home.

You inhale sharp as the broken glass that surrounds you. The black velvet curtain falls—a loud snap, a clatter, then smoke. Shadow-you turns with open palms. You place the quill in her hand and when you touch her, you ignite, alive and crackling. You turn back to see the nest once more but the glass is gone, the nest, the bird, your father. Your yearning for one more word is so familiar you can't help but reach for it and start to scream, but Shadow-you, quill in hand, catches your arm and pulls you back. Your scars shiver as your patterns reconfigure a new structure. Your mouth is helpless, open, and Shadow-you places her lips over yours, then whispers,

"A tumor always eats its host. We must kill the host to kill the tumor. Are you dead yet, my love? Did you uncover and destroy the food you offered Death?"

I fed it you, Daddy. I fed it our home—the red-shuttered house on the rolling hill. The okra and the butter beans. The creek with the alligator, your life unlived. I fed it you.

Raven

I am gone.

Me

You are gone.

"But you are here," says Shadow-you as she draws your breath into hers and you deflate, the last grief-filled helium balloon set free among the trees, and when you step out of rubbered skin, bare toes spread wide, and press them onto soft brown carpet, your inhale startles the edges of your throat. You cough, your tongue moving up and down, back and forth against the dark wet cavern of your mouth. Salt from sea to sea pours from your eyes into an hourglass set center on your desk. You turn it, watch the grains begin to slide.

Living is a commitment.

You push new words past your lips:
I am here. Daddy, you are there.
The hourglass fills bottom to top.

The next time I turn it,
I'll be home.

ACKNOWLEDGEMENTS

So many people's hearts went into helping me create this book. In no particular order: Gayle Brandeis, Michaela Carter, and Rick Hamilton, for being gracious early readers and helping me find coherence and continuity; Alma Luz Villanueva for encouraging me twenty years ago to write the scene I couldn't write until 2019; Jim Natal for hosting my first reading and conversation from the book and always being in my literary corner; Linda Roghaar, my agent since 2003, who has always supported my "weird unclassifiable projects"; Jaynie Royal and the team at Regal House for understanding my vision for this work and believing in it enough to champion it; Chelsey Clammer, editor extraordinaire who took this book from dumpster fire to something I couldn't have envisioned without her; Ariel Gore, who inspired the book with one of her Saturday Morning Prompts and has helped me embrace all of my weird; the wonderful Wayward Writers who gave me feedback along the way, especially Jenny Forrester, Laura Cline, and Meg Weber. Lidia Yuknavitch, whom I only met once, and I froze up when I shook her hand, but whose work thawed me, and Dalena Watson, who has helped me uncover and release more creatures from my psyche than anyone else on earth.

And to Keith, my person, who listened to me read every word of every draft out loud and never once fell asleep.

Author's Note

A book like this one doesn't come to be without some negotiations. I knew I was taking a risk combining two disparate formats together into a whole, and I knew I was compounding that risk by adding the word "speculative" in front of the word "memoir." Why not just call it a novel? Well, because it isn't one. This book is accurate, in the ways that a memoir is "true" through the blurred lens of its author. I have not deliberately lied or provided misinformation or compressed events in this story. My memory, though, is as fallible as yours, and I expect other people have different perspectives.

I have always inhabited the world through a touch of magic. I'm the one who names appliances and cars and bicycles. The one who forms intense relationships with houses and carries old photographs of people I don't know from place to place because I can't bear for no one to see their faces anymore. I am more than a touch witchy, and I gravitated to fiction first because it was a place I could plant all my ghosts. But then those ghosts stretched into my regular life, and to write non-fiction without including the very elements that make my own life's lens sparkle would have been the biggest lie of all.

Did my father actually come to the backyard as a talking raven? Not literally. But Barnessa the cat did! And there really was a message on my answering machine from my father, two years after he died.

The prompt that inspired the book came from Ariel Gore: *Write me a story. Someone important to you who has died has not died. They knock at your door. And you show them around your current life. Somewhere in this story, show your visitor a book.* I tried having Dad come back as Dad, but it was just strange. Yes, stranger than what this book turned into! But when I had him arrive as a raven, the whole book cracked open. And then, with the help of Chelsey Clammer, I found Raven's voice—a mix of poetic forms and staccato sounds. It was in a channeled state during a music therapy session where I saw the structure of the book as two towers: a lyrical, linear storyline, and then an archetypal storyline, dramatized as a stage play. In the beginning, the two worlds are more starkly separate, but as the book progresses, the forms begin to merge into a true hybrid, representing an integration of the external and internal realms we all inhabit.

The lyric essays that make up one tower are "true". The archetypal storyline is also "true", with the exception of actual talking ravens—though I do live in northern Arizona where there are murders of ravens chattering everywhere. All the things Raven, Raven's Mother, Raven's Father, and Me discuss in the Ancestral Realm were things that happened in our family. I imagined the characters' inner worlds based on my experiences with them while they were living and the stories of other family members.

Trauma can be inherited, and the dead are not static. I realized that much of what was emerging in my body after I was diagnosed with cancer wasn't my own grief, but the grief of my ancestors, and because I'm a writer, the only thing I knew to do was to use language to write us all home. Every word in this book originated from love and from a belief in the power of forgiveness and grace. And yes, my mother read the whole thing on a trip we took to New York City!

I have a younger sister, Melanie, who has explicitly requested not to be included in anything I write, so I have respected that. It's not always a welcome thing to have a sister who is a writer. She does know that I'm mentioning her name here, and she knows what the book is about, though she doesn't appear in the pages.

I chose speculative memoir because that is the most authentic form for how I see the world. I chose a stage play format for the archetypal arc because the dead are so often disembodied voices in our lives, and I felt disembodied when I was navigating cancer. A black box theatre set seemed most appropriate for that world, and I wanted enough space for the characters to fly away when they were done.

Thank you for taking time to visit with my ghosts, and may you remember to tend to your own.

Laraine Herring, May 14, 2020